Hypn...

How to Deepen Hypnosis With Hypnotic Fractionation

(A Comprehensive Guide to Erotic Hypnosis and Relyfe Programming)

Buster McLaughlin

Published By **Darby Connor**

Buster McLaughlin

All Rights Reserved

Hypnosis: How to Deepen Hypnosis With Hypnotic Fractionation (A Comprehensive Guide to Erotic Hypnosis and Relyfe Programming)

ISBN 978-1-998927-16-6

I almost pay attention you pronouncing, "Well, I've in no manner been hypnotized" or "It might no longer be capable of hypnotize me." I can nearly pay attention what you're going to mention subsequent.

Have you in no way been on an elevator, only to understand a while later that you got off at the wrong floor, best to right now get lower once more on the elevator while you realized your mistake?

Or, have you ever ever been the use of a vehicle on a acquainted route for an extended distance after which found out that for a large term you were not conscious that you have been driving, that you do not preserve in thoughts passing positive landmarks on the street, and that your thoughts has been some other place clearly? Have you ever had this enjoy?

Or, have you ever ever ever never been so preoccupied with some thing else which you forgot someone become speaking to you for a long time, most effective to understand afterwards that you ignored it clearly? You might also have stated some issue along the strains of "my thoughts drifted."

However, which have become like being under the have an impact on of hypnosis. Your mind did now not "adventure" everywhere; it's far despite the fact that inside the identical region inside your head as it have grow to be before.

The Working Relationship Between Hypnosis and NLP

It is idea that you are more receptive to hints that can be of use to you whilst you are on this dream u.S., that is wherein an professional practitioner of hypnotism and NLP can function you.

To flow into beforehand with the procedure, we require every your cooperation and your willingness to get handled.

Any inspiration which you perform a little issue which you discover revolting or offensive will fast supply out that dreamer's e-statistic, or "trance," as hypnotists call it. [Citation needed] [Citation needed]

The most proficient hypnotist of our time

Richard Bandler, a co-founding father of neuro-linguistic programming (NLP), is appreciably seemed as one of the most talented hypnotists despite the fact that energetic these days. Both hypnotism and NLP are among his areas of knowledge.

Richard Bandler changed right into a pc modeler and graduate student on the time that he collaborated with John Grinder, a professor on the group, so that it will determine the traits of genius in significantly talented people.

The pioneer of present day clinical hypnosis, Milton H. Erickson, MD, changed into this type of humans. The scientific global became left in a nation of misunderstanding with the aid of Erickson's prowess and achievements.

They were able to piece collectively Erickson's pretty complicated behavior at the same time as he modified into developing hypnotic states of interest via their blended efforts.

On the opportunity hand, they discovered that their actions accompanied unique patterns and have been prepared in a superb manner at the equal time.

No part of this guidebook shall be reproduced in any form without permission in writing from the publisher except in the case of brief quotations embodied in critical articles or reviews.

Legal & Disclaimer

The information contained in this book is not designed to replace or take the place of any form of medicine or professional medical advice. The information in this book has been provided for educational & entertainment purposes only.

The information contained in this book has been compiled from sources deemed reliable, and it is accurate to the best of the Author's knowledge; however, the Author cannot guarantee its accuracy and validity and cannot be held liable for any errors or omissions. Changes are periodically made to this book. You must consult your doctor or get professional medical advice before using any of the suggested remedies, techniques, or information in this book.

Upon using the information contained in this book, you agree to hold harmless the Author from and against any damages, costs, and expenses, including any legal fees potentially resulting from the application of any of the information provided by this guide. This disclaimer applies to any damages or injury caused by the use and application, whether directly or indirectly, of any advice or information presented, whether for breach of contract, tort, negligence, personal injury, criminal intent, or under any other cause of action.

You agree to accept all risks of using the information presented inside this book. You need to consult a professional medical practitioner in order to ensure you are both able and healthy enough to participate in this program.

Table Of Contents

Chapter 1: Luring & Influencing 'Friends'

In times of emotional, economic, and romantic struggles we obtain out to our friends for comfort. After all, we've got a connection with them that we don't with mere strangers we brush past in the road.

In our time of need, we are able to count on them to help us overcome whatever limitations are our way. Yet, the fact is that we don't surely understand our pals the least bit.

They aren't us, and we aren't them. Within the privacy of their very very own minds, a wildly various creature with many man or woman components dwells. It longs to show itself to others but is aware of it need to stay hidden due to the fact self-protection is the important thing riding force to all human behaviour.

As particular people, we may also bond over commonplace interests with our buddies.

But whilst the chips are down and everything is on the road, them otherwise you, they'll sacrifice you without hesitation to preserve themselves.

All of Us Are Narcissists.

When we're more youthful our narcissism plays out within the shape of our self-image. We end up obsessed by the use of how we look to others and the manner they perceive our splendor. Do they fancy us? Do they need to kiss me?

As adults, this narcissism takes the shape of the testimonies we tell ourselves. Perhaps we trust we're strangely practical, or an above-average commonplace motive force or a in particular moral character. Our opinions are wherein we are looking for the maximum validation due to the fact they may be a forex of our rate to others.

In our primitive tribe thoughts, it's crucial that we're favored and valued for our exciting and principled stance we tackle current affairs or social problems. None people can undergo the perception of being sturdy out from the company and being left to rot in isolation and insignificance.

This narcissism ensures that we rightfully region a barrier among ourselves and others. The final element we want is for humans to recognise who we actually are. After all, it's dangerous for us to reveal our actual selves to others. It's in reality a existence or loss of life situation.

The beginning of master manipulation is to get others to assist you to into their minds. Appealing to their narcissism is a clean get right of entry to issue to influencing them in a few manner. The way to get others to drop their natural defences is to reflect them. Declare the same pastimes, dress like them and rage toward a commonplace enemy.

What people like extra than their personal opinions and thoughts are specific individuals who mirror and embody them. Better than listening to their very personal opinion is being attentive to you verify and laud their opinion. This validates them as a human and that they start to relax. They turn out to be open to you because you aren't a risk - you are not the opportunity.

This lowering of the defend is in reality an invite an first rate way to walk into the fort and to begin chipping down their walls from the indoors, one piece at a time.

As time progresses you may have an effect on them collectively at the side of your very non-public reviews and thoughts from a place of solidified rapport and perceived mutual respect.

They will be aware of you because of the reality you are a friend - a person who they see a chunk of themselves in, which they love almost extra than some thing. It offers them a sense of belonging and the perception that collectively, you're every superior to everyone else.

Little do they apprehend that they'll be taking naps inside the jaws of a wonderful white shark.

Utilize Laughter as Your Trojan Horse

Stand-up comedians use laughter as a manner to get their factor at some point of. Jokes lighten up the aware mind enough in order that the subconscious mind has a smooth course to concentrate to the mind and pointers encoded in their jokes.

Once you get another person to giggle, they're more likely to preserve guffawing. Use sarcasm and humorous observations as an opportunity to interact an energetic listener. This doesn't suggest turning your self right into a court docket jester or class clown. This is a brief manner to lose respect and impact over someone due to the truth those roles have the bottom social reputation.

5

Subtle however normal humour indicators to them which you 'get' the arena and that you're 'with them'. Their laughter relaxes them sufficient simply so they're primed to take in your worldwide view.

The fact is that people have a propensity to be horrible listeners. Most humans are sincerely looking for their turn to talk rather than processing what's being stated with the useful useful resource of the opportunity man or woman in a communique. Laughter is precise. People want to snicker and in the event that they suppose someone is perceptually funny, they'll draw close on every phrase that they're saying.

Use this for your benefit. Use humour as a manner to mock those you preference to freeze out. Isolate them and choose out out their flaws. Embarrass them in a subtle way, through 'banter'.

This mild-hearted method is a first rate manner to steer your 'pals' round in your considering who they ought to probably forged aside. Your sharp wit exposes a member of the institution who is the subsequent in line to be choked out – make this person your rival.

It moreover acts as a moderate reminder to those 'pals' which may be guffawing, that they could with out issues be next want to they fail to live in your real aspect. The unusual calm immoderate-reputation comedian has a uniquely powerful grip on any enterprise business enterprise.

Play Dumb

Nobody likes to experience stupid. Baking within the glare of judging eyes surely burns your shallowness. At excessive excellent elements on your lifestyles being the dumb one is inevitable, even in case you are actively stopping this. There's no getting a long way from it - there'll constantly be all people smarter than you. Accept this reality of lifestyles however turn this occasional vulnerable issue into an advantage.

To avoid feeling much like the stupid one in the room, maximum humans pass via lifestyles appearing intellectually advanced to others. This may fit on activities however it's one of the super strategies to lose friends.

As a grasp manipulator, you could need to say your power and monitor your superiority - however that comes later down the line at the same time as you are getting towards the throne. When you are in a rather powerless position, you want to attract and then maintain those equal friends.

At each opportunity, subtly feed into someone's perception that they may be greater clever than you. This disarms them and they're no longer possibly to see you as a danger. After all, how can a far less smart individual ever get the higher of them?

This doesn't advocate you need to faux to be of notably a good deal less intelligence. You really want to make it obvious which you don't pursue analyzing. Books don't interest you and who cares what's taking place in the global? You are handiest a harmless individual dedicated to a friendship where you could share fulfilling moments with them - whilst every so often bowing to their first-rate mind.

This 'natural order' you're filing to makes them experience better approximately themselves and feeds their ego. Of path, that when humans have low expectancies of you, you have were given an opportunity to run amok in conjunction with your smart video video games of manipulation.

Conceal your True Intentions

It's so clean to get humans speakme about themselves. At coronary coronary heart, we are all narcissists truely searching ahead to our flip to talk. There is a yearning in us all to talk our 'fact'. We want our opinions to be heard and then have them established so we're able to experience a quick-time period ounce of self confidence.

Just take a look at the general go along with the drift of your common conversation - one person talks about their issues, their reviews on contemporary affairs and their hopes for his or her destiny. Just a informal question for the purpose of performing well mannered can elicit strangers to expose their darkest secrets and techniques and strategies or grasp plan for their destiny.

As a grasp manipulator, you want to not fall into this entice. You, my pal, are notable. You see, even as human beings show their hopes and dreams, they will be actually begging to be manipulated.

You don't need to be at the receiving stop of manipulation. By withholding your real intentions, you maintain your energy. Nobody can use your desires closer to you in the event that they don't recognise what they're. It takes effort to hold your tongue and now not fall for the bait of nosey people but live controlled within the statistics that you develop ever powerful with each passing self-restraint.

When humans pick out to be so open, it makes them predictable and no longer viable to recognize. Train your self in the art of concealment if you have any choice for real energy over the ones spherical you.

It's normal for optimum humans to just accept appearances for the sake of maintaining their non-public sanity. If one is to live in a global wherein they need to continuously query the motive of others, they will rapid sink into madness and paranoia.

You alternatively are one-of-a-type. Manipulation is part of the game of lifestyles and actual power is residing inside the shadows. It's from the shadows that you need to function in case you need to dominate your international.

This does not suggest you need to constantly be manifestly secretive. No, this can flip humans off from you. Too a whole lot thriller frustrates human beings and pushes them away. You even though need to show your intentions, simply now not your real ones.

Reveal faux plans and dreams which might be despite the fact that in shape for greatness however hard to recognize the records or define a unique course than the most effective you are certainly pursuing. Remember, statistics is king, and your fighters can be looking for methods to apply it in the route of you.

Those who're playing a game such as you, in search of to apply your intentions towards you can then be distracted by means of time-ingesting galivants - leaving you by myself for your real pursuit. Be honest in your 'honest revelation of your intentions.

Also, at the identical time because the opportunity arises, make it identified to every person which you hold honesty because the very high-quality price. Not quality do you hold your self to that desired, however you call for it from others. This virtuous reputation ensures that nobody will ever suspect you of concealment and manipulative campaigns of disinformation.

Mirror to Build Rapport

An powerful manner of concealing your real intentions is to reflect your desires. Mirrors are greater deceptive than we like to assume. They are a beneficial manner to look ourselves, yet they coax us into overlooking components of appearance that we dislike. By encouraging us to cognizance on certain elements of our our our bodies, they fail to expose us how others see us.

When you replicate any other individual, you achieve this with the aid of the usage of reflecting their beliefs, opinions, and values over again at them. You seduce them through inflating their very very personal ego further to manufacturing a experience which you every percentage a robust and proper connection. Both of you're birds of a feather who have to consequently stick collectively.

In our loopy international, it's unusual that we enjoy we are truely seen and therefore understood with the aid of others. So while it does occur, we phrase this particular 2nd and adhere onto it for a long time afterwards.

Mirroring is a effective way of manipulating nearly truely anybody. Few have the mental wherewithal to stand up to such draw close manipulation magick.

Give Before you Take

Selective honesty can be a bug that breaches the defence of even the maximum guarded individual. It's difficult to mistrust a person who is being 'sincere'. Selective honesty works because of the reality it is a distraction as is what we recognize to be generosity.

Tech giants like Google and Facebook have given us the energy to pursue limitless statistics and 'connection'. Even now, anyways that has been written and stated their darkish reasons, there are however a few folks that don't apprehend that their company isn't a random, sincere act of generosity.

As most dad and mom understand by using now, the ones organizations are corporations. Their purpose is for maximum profits and energy. In go back for our loose use in their provider, we surrender our private statistics and with it, our humanity. So plenty so, that they apprehend us higher than we apprehend ourselves. Their ever-evolving complex algorithms understand and target our character regular styles.

This AI does this with cold, rational exquisite judgment and is unaffected with the aid of some thing tales we are deciding on to keep in mind approximately ourselves and the region.

You can art work this generosity fact to you gain. People want things and that they opt for it while a few factor that they choice is 'loose'. As narcissists, arrogance and validation are what we are seeking out. Give them exactly that - an sudden praise it absolutely is both honest and specific.

You don't like them due to their appropriate nature - you need them due to the fact they are exceptional sons, daughters and companions. They aren't in reality bodily attractive humans - the heady scent of their fragrance makes you need to bark like a dog or they've an incredible eye for clothes and add-ons.

Selective kindness is a calculated way to play on someone's emotions and need to be special. Everybody likes to accumulate gadgets because it throws us another time proper into a childlike u . S . A .. This childlike surprise created through unexpected generosity makes it tough for them to be suspicious or dislike you.

Chapter 2: Seduction

When it includes manipulating those with who you are romantically concerned (or need to be romantically concerned), seduction is your simplest device. The capability to seduce one or multiple humans at any given time is the very last direction to manipulation mastery.

When beginning out on your adventure you want to simply take delivery of the simple fact: Everybody desires to be seduced. All humans are begging to be manipulated (under fake pretences if need be) into some thing that represents a actual-lifestyles love spell.

Our innate sexual impulses lie at the foundation of everything that we do in our society. Being excellent, well mannered and virtuous are all truely covers for in search of to expose up our actual goals which is probably typically sexual in nature.

Everything comes all of the manner down to sex. Everybody feels this - you aren't on my own in feeling this too. You are everyday, similar to every person else.

Some enjoy it greater than others of path. It's commonplace for people to pursue sexual relations however the reality that they recognize that it's going to motive their coronary coronary heart being damaged.

Harness this clean reality of life and you can manage the area round you as you please.

Design Attention Triangles

Our society's consumerist inclinations display off that some difficulty becomes extra valuable if it's far favored through way of a person else aside from you. This is how belongings charges are driven up; a place has pinnacle climate, lots of services and brilliant houses - consequently every person desires to stay there, and fees rise due to this.

You can create this level of competition for your very very personal social circle. The traditional manner of doing that is to create triangles, putting yourself centrally due to the fact the seemed item of desire. Desirability is a social illusion which may be cultivated at your will.

To acquire fulfillment at becoming the most best character to your social organization, you need to manage with cause. You want to create an phantasm that you are in fact, the most crucial person inside the room with the very first-rate social popularity. You do this, through showing humans glimpses of your significance within the small moments.

This isn't about usually being the centre of attention or wearing the brightest clothes. It's about growing an air of secrecy which you are great in order that humans short stop that they could not straight away benefit from your excessive tatus, truely with the useful resource of being spherical you.

Desire is aggressive. We need what others need and we want it at their rate. As kids we sought out our determine's hobby - we wanted it more than our siblings. Remember, we are all narcissists who want to come returned first. A way we will collect this need is to collect what different humans choice, to show that we're worth.

Let human beings chase your valuable hobby at the manner to live out their narcissistic fantasies of being the selected one. Do this via surrounding yourself with buddies and spouse and children of the opportunity sex even as out in public. From a distance, this gives others a signal which you are genuinely absolutely well worth others time and interest.

Leveraging this effective device of social approval immediately will increase your social capital, a key guiding precept of attracting the ones from the opposite and same intercourse who can come to be excellent belongings to you.

Allow those for your inner circle to get near you however maintain decrease returned from ever certainly giving your self over to others. As well as showing individuals who are out of doors of your inner circle that there are humans preventing over you, this technique continues subjects clean inside the internal circle itself.

The revel in that an inner circle competitor is getting greater hobby is insufferable for human beings. From the centre, you could entice humans in with their conceitedness after which strike them down because of it.

Be open about it. Give brief hobby to at the least one character, then randomly take it away and vicinity it on their competitor.

This doesn't want to be a competitor within the maximum real enjoy of the word, it can be their personal terrific pal, a sibling or perhaps their good-looking discern who has tested a unethical to need to incorporate themselves of their little one's affairs. This is the way you create a triangle to excellent impact.

It's the manner you create mass hysteria on a micro social degree, enthusiastic about your very very very very own advantage. Be your personal PR agent. Quietly building up your very private popularity after which unleash the chaos.

Then you can retreat for your immoderate horse steady within the information which you have won, regardless of how the subsequent drama performs out.

Find their 'lack of'

Our egos are a tremendous deal more fragile than we lead others to don't forget. Everybody wears many mask in an try to conceal their right feelings out of worry of being lessen loose from the tribe. Normally, those actual emotions that we tough to apprehend are specifically made of anxieties, low arrogance and confusion on the which means of existence.

These everyday neurotic competencies which can be conventional at some point of all cultures, are super assets on your try to manipulate at will. As a draw near manipulator, you want to in no way take a person's study face rate.

Everybody you stumble upon might also have fears, doubts and traumas lurking below their carefully curated outdoor. Even the maximum assured people you stumble upon are that manner for a few purpose. Comedians crave the attention they felt they in no way had been given as a little one.

Many CEO's and entrepreneurs are running far from childhoods of shortage or are pushed thru the crushing expectancies in their a success mother and father. 'People Pleasers' will be inclined to have continual self-esteem troubles and models have grown up under the relentless glare of unwanted interest and harsh judgement.

Everybody has developed from a specific 'lack of', and it's your interest to discover what this is. Once you installation this, you have your golden fee fee ticket to ruthlessly make the most them in the quality way possible: You offer them what they want and motive them to revel in ok about a burden they have been sporting by myself for their complete lives.

You undergo witness to their suffering, and you offer them place to talk in self belief to you. Once they display their reality, possibly for the primary time ever, that's if you have them. They turn out to be putty in your arms – equipped to be squeezed and moulded in any manner which you see in shape.

To try this, you typically have to 'move first', as in you need to show your 'truth' to them.

Of course, this isn't your actual 'truth'. You need to in no manner display your very very very own fears, doubts and insecurities to anybody due to the fact this is the way you cede your very own power.

No, your 'reality' ia s meditated photo in their personal fact, the one you need them to tell you and most effective you. So you need to were observing them and function a feel for what sort of deep dark mystery they'll be shielding directly to.

Once you get them to say this out loud, an without delay bond is created. This bond isn't always equal, but, as you are the simplest who has pulled the strings and extracted their vulnerabilities. Normally, they may enjoy visible and heard for the very first time.

If this man or woman is a capability romantic accomplice, they'll grow to be proper away interested by you. This is a exceptional time to make a circulate. If it's a pal or member of the family, your grip on their devotion becomes more impregnable and extra exciting for each activities, particularly you.

Create Temptation

Remember, maximum people stay mundane lives of quiet desperation. They live for the weekend, grinding their way via their semi-meaningless jobs to move another time to their static dating, or to raise their traumatic households. They in all likelihood sense an excessive amount of pressure and now not severa appreciation, especially girls.

You apprehend that it must be laborious for them to keep order even as their inner turmoil indicates that they in truth live in international of chaos. Our 'moral' society prospers off an unstated collective settlement that we need to repress our desires due to the reality they're wrong.

As a draw close manipulator you can prey on the ocean of worn-out souls who litter the streets. You can create temptation and then dangle it within the the front of them just like the ray of mild (or darkest demon) that they have been longing for.

Perhaps they prolonged to 'permit their hair down' and overlook about about their duties for as soon as. Or perhaps they have a taboo myth which has been eating them up.

Whatever it's far, they secretly want to yield to it. Even if they are too uncomfortable to inform their near ones, if you could create a robust enough temptation in a 'consistent' surroundings for them to relent to their impulses, then you may be the only to build up their passionate gratitude.

By lifting the veil on their darkest, maximum repressed goals, you manipulate them into becoming enthusiastic about you. After all, you're supplying them with psychosexual recovery of the private kind.

Keep them off Balance

Creating suspense and maintaining a experience of mystery succeeds at maintaining your purpose off stability. By failing to follow a habitual and proudly rejecting cultural expectancies, you could gasoline an obsession inside the different person.

This obsession is borne out of a continual enjoy of surprise, confusion, and admiration. The further you could lead them off beam, the crazier their global will appear to them.

The further you encourage them to benefit into their shadow, the extra emotional they get. They will go away rational thinking inside the again of and begin to live greater inside the present 2d. As a calculated manipulator, living within the present 2nd fits you because you are on pinnacle of things of these 'moments'.

Your regular trade of plan and disdain for habitual ensures that you call the pix. The similarly away they are drawn from 'normality', the greater intoxicated they become - with you.

Promise a Surprise Gift

When someone is promised a wonder, their electricity of mind straight away reduces. After all, you are approximately to provide them a gift - however what's going to or no longer it's far?

Randomly handing them a gift is okay and can courier short favour to you. However, telling them they will gather one in some days or possibly weeks will preserve the spell you preserve over them.

This future date, wherein a tremendous possibility awaits them, is a much greater powerful shape of manipulation. It takes them decrease lower back to their formative years while there was a greater revel in of what can be completed in existence. As we flow into into adulthood this enjoy of optimism is hard to preserve because the drudgery of life grinds us down.

By reigniting that enjoy of wonder, you engrain yourself due to the truth the maximum vital and interesting man or woman of their lifestyles.

Resistance is an Invitation

Encountering resistance inside the manipulative pursuit of some different individual is often a accurate signal. It is everyday for human beings to surrender and flow without delay to another intention if the character they're targeted on makes a big deal about how they'll be able to't deliver in to these 'unwanted' advances.

If you're deep right into a manipulative pursuit and also you meet such dramatic resistance, appreciate their obstacles however you can probable maintain to pursue them. Such presentations show that the person's emotions are engaged in terms of you - a inform-tale signal that your manipulation is strolling.

As lengthy due to the fact the enchantment is mutual, it probably manner that they're at the cusp to in reality giving themselves over to you.

In this case, you may want to be creative in your tries to finish your seductive manipulation. Doing some thing unexpected will paintings wonders. Perhaps you will be distinctly generous or perform a courageous act in a hard scenario.

Whether the scenario is actually unstable or a synthetic scare, by dashing in because of the truth the not unusual-or-lawn hero you'll create the greater area of protection for them to completely put up to their feelings for you.

Often folks who play the characteristic of the resistor are checking out human beings to look who will upward thrust to the event. That character may be you, even if you control the state of affairs so the chances are stacked firmly for your favour.

You can also control the PR of your heroic act through way of the usage of physical demonstrating how plenty you 'placed on the street'. If it doesn't paintings immediately, all is not out of place - you can unfold stories of your bravery to others who weren't present simply so phrase of your heroic deeds begin to flow into.

Play the Role of Therapist

Transference is an hassle all therapists and psychiatrists face. It's a phenomenon that they're informed to try to keep away from in which in any respect possible in order that the expert and moral traces do not grow to be blurred. As a draw close manipulator, you can use this famous reality of life on your devilish gain.

As maximum intellectual neurosis can be traced again to formative years, that is the herbal course that verbal exchange in a recuperation putting can also take. Using cautious questioning the therapist slowly gets the affected person to stable their minds once more to their childhood.

As youngsters we're essentially powerless and certainly counting on our dad and mom. Due to the irrational expectancies we've got were given of our dad and mom even as kids, they necessarily disappoint us. As we come to be antique this pain can take place into an entire host of mental disturbances.

Yet however this, it's now not unusual for us to look lower back right proper into a past thru rose-tinted glasses.

We prolonged for the approval of our dad or mum that we may think we by no means have been given. Or we unconsciously are looking for decision to our feelings of misconception we professional because of the fact the darkish nature of the sector have end up obvious to us.

You can harness the ones deep afflictions which lurk underneath the floor in everyone. When in quiet, constant situations, you could carefully manual your aim into regression through calculated communique.

Your attentive listening and interest of their beyond shows that you are traumatic and interested by them. You need to remain calm and comparatively quiet - in a way, you need to continue to be emotionally cold and unflinching to any horrors they display.

Let them sit down down of their own neuroses as they mentally entangle themselves. As they sense the push of feelings from their faraway past, they look to the easy canvas you're growing and transfer their love (and longing) for his or her parents onto you.

There is not any love stronger than that of discern and toddler. By effectively setting your self in that feature within the eyes of another, you turn out to be the centre in their universe.

During those extreme and intimate conversations, it's commonplace for snippets of information to be observed out which you may then use later down the street. Be conscious even though, no longer the entirety that they may be announcing goes to be gospel fact or goal. Memories may be unreliable and tainted.

Look for modifications in their tonality as they speak, or unexpected micro anxiety of their frame. Take study of subjects they dance spherical. These are clues that some element deliver of ache they've, you ought to show them to cement their emotional attachment to you.

A individual will once in a while make statements that are the direct contrary of the way they in fact revel in. If they'll be announcing they 'hate' their mother as an example, it will usually suggest they extended for her love and be close to her, however experience they've got now not skilled this for something purpose. The word hate usually suggests love. When someone is bored, they're generally unhappy, sad or angry. When a person is angry, they may be in all likelihood unhappy and on and on. Rarely will we talk at once while feeling emotionally charged or susceptible.

As this form of truth comes out, you may control your price via the usage of way of positioning your self to fill this therapist characteristic. Remember, motive them to revel in steady and heard at the way to undertaking their love without delay to you.

Stimulate Feelings of Anxiety

Boredom kills libido. The monotony of ordinary, mundane life is a trap that maximum people are trapped into. As a grasp manipulator, you can make someone obsess over you by means of introducing drama into their lives.

It's everyday for the commonplace character to be unfalteringly prone and due to their pathetic tendencies, they default to 'gambling the sufferer'. Most humans are going round because the primary man or woman within the film of their very very personal lifestyles. Bizarrely, in this film, they are a selecting to play a person that is being victimized time and again.

This is really one instance of approaches irrational all people is. You can manipulate them into feelings of infatuation via manner of giving them exactly what they appear to want. If they see themselves as a sufferer, address them like one.

Be cruel. Unleash your verbal aggression onto them through telling them just how traumatic you find them. Threaten to withdraw your hobby and bodily leave in case you want to.

If you are uncertain of wherein to start, recognition on what small topics also can annoy you approximately them and simply roll with that. The fear and anxiety you create out of your unforgiving revelation of truth will cause them to feel alive, likely for the primary time in a long term. They are surely engaged in a conflict of types, and you are their arch enemy.

By in no way permitting them to end up too cushty, you preserve a perpetual state of 'what if'. Fear of abandonment and crushing loss will strength someone into doing all they are able to to preserve you. They will do some thing it takes to maintain you and you will be able to ask for what you need.

Capture Their Spirit

If you choice to take your manipulation of a romantic associate to awesome tiers, you need to invoke the spiritual nature of existence. Pleasure and ache are the number one tiers of manipulation, but you have to seize their soul if you need to strike a 'as quickly as in a (their) lifetime' bond.

Nothing is greater powerful at this than the attraction of the mystical and unseen.

It's essential that you insinuate that there are hidden mystical depths to you which of them may be geared up to be positioned out. This can be some thing from your hobby in spirituality, the mystical, magick or astronomy.

There's no better manner to draw the emotionally bored and at risk of you than to trace at a capacity new reality it is infinitely extra first-rate than their cutting-edge life. They in reality want to provide themselves over to you to gain get right of access to into this unseen fact.

Use art work as a tool to control them into questioning thoughts of the divine. Take them to an art work gallery or a grand constructing where deep conversations begin without trouble.

Even higher is to go on my own beforehand and find a bit of paintings that you think may resonate with them. As you glide round collectively, take them to the perfect piece that 'reminded you of them'. Of direction, this doesn't want to be real or valid - it clearly need to be tailored sufficient to their very very own non-public tastes.

In a international in which order is prioritised over chaos, you could introduce spiritual chaos into the existence of your chosen motive. Speculate that future is at artwork and that a higher strength is pulling the strings.

Perhaps you could interest on your 'meeting of minds' and how it isn't always unintended.

The magic of the universe is at paintings and neither you nor your aim has a proper to forestall what activities the cosmos has set into motion.

As they end up intoxicated inside the spiritual myth you have got were given weaved, you want to normalise the scenario of sexuality into your conversation. Make it perfectly clear which you remember intercourse to be an wonderful demonstration of your passion for each one-of-a-kind.

Don't keep lower once more for your preference to fulfil your romantic future and be bold to your movements. Once their spirit is now inner your hold close, you're in the correct position to make your waft.....In the end... the celebs are aligned and the Gods have spoken!

Cultivate Jealousy

When someone is jealous, they lose sight of their rational minds and get stuck up in a sense of heightened emotion. At factors of pinnacle manipulation, you could have someone absolutely beside themselves with raging jealousy – or no much less than, envy which you may use in your advantage.

A jealous individual's lack of smooth mindedness lends itself to your pursuit of getting what you need. If they're acting frantically and appear determined for your interest or reassurance, provide it to them, conditionally.

Make positive they see that you have loads of various (and probable) better alternatives than them. Clearly deliver that better popularity options are available to you, and you can decide to direct your interest and affection to them in area of your frantic admirer in the event that they do now not comply with your situations.

Then, keep the danger of your cross lower back, so long as they agree to your new phrases. They will neither refuse to negotiate.

Chapter 3: Personal War & Enacting Your Grand Masterplan for Total Domination

Everything Changes

In a worldwide it's fluid and ever converting, committing to an entrenched feature in any stroll of life is mostly a catastrophically bypass. There is not any price in tying yourself to an internal set of values.

Nothing extremely good can be performed in case you pathetically hold close to a inflexible ideology.

The worldwide is essentially from your control however the manner you pick out out to conform can be important on your successes or failures. You need to pass through lifestyles seeking to be as happily seamless as possible. You need to be the most fluid individual for your circle.

A grasp manipulators lengthy workout is complicated and requires a devious diploma of pleasant staying strength and making plans. Instead of habitually looking to aggressively take the throne at the primary opportunity, it serves you higher to carefully encircle your desires so that they don't have any clue of your threatening technique.

Being fluid technique which you must be organized to sometimes surrender your feature within the knowledge which you are playing a larger exercise. Don't allow your vanity trick you into stopping losing battles. Losses are to be expected when you are preventing a battle.

Your power must be conserved for the larger game and additional importantly, your true cause need to continue to be concealed and real in your deep desires.

Aggression has its place. It need to be a device for your arsenal however handiest utilised all through the final act, to decisively complete your big endeavor of manipulation. At this element, your goal might be no longer capable of resist this ruthless act because of the reality they're in a feel of perilous confusion

Prior to this point, your method need to be primarily based on not standing nonetheless. Your game of manipulation ought to no longer seem obvious - it wishes to be an indirect approach based totally totally on loosely associated dots.

Never take some thing in my view or it may be used in competition to you over and over. Appear flexible to changing plans and don't become known as a person who is awkward and rigid within the converting panorama.

You are a person who can't be damage. Remain smiling and terrific in the face of any surprising inconvenience which can upward thrust up. Appear to conform whilst studiously walking behind the scenes to do what you want to.

Share a Secret

Everybody has weaknesses with a number of them being extra wicked and lurid than others. Whilst many people are brief to speak without end approximately themselves in the hunt for validation, it's despite the fact that unusual for sincere revelations of the deepest kind.

As we broaden out of our youth, the painful fact of the area we stay in turns into greater obvious with each passing day. We understand that our parents in the long run can't guard us from the difficult realities of lifestyles. Despite their (with a bit of luck) incredible intentions, they cannot shield us from demise, contamination and worst of all: extreme social judgement that consequences in us becoming a pariah.

Perhaps most humans's worse worry is that they may be rejected through their friends. For this cause, we maintain what we apprehend to be our personal flaws (real or not) from others.

Over time these secrets can placed on us down. A new preference arises, in which we long for the day that we're capable of offload the name of the game which has come to be a heavy burden on our tired shoulders. Still, we recognise higher than to broadcast our 'weaknesses'.

As a keep close manipulator, your reason is to realise as many secrets and techniques and techniques as feasible - particularly the ones folks that are targets of yours. This is a tough assignment but no longer as hard as it may appear. A simple truth will do the trick regardless of the fact that.

Readily offer up your very very own 'secret' to this person on the facts that they have to defend it with their life. The thriller doesn't want to be real of route - in fact, it shouldn't. It must be a fabricated one which carefully resembles what you consider to be theirs (if possible).

People display their reality constantly. Although maximum people will not openly nation their deepest secrets and techniques and strategies, their our bodies betray them as the overall topics of verbal exchange that they belong to are spoken of. Their hands, eyes and toes will tap uncontrollably or bodily as they may be looking to get via the modern uncomfortable 2d they discover themselves in.

Work your way thru your suspicions earlier than taking reason. You don't want to be one hundred% accurate however it is able to most effective useful aid your cause whilst the big second of revelation arrives.

There are two number one forms of deep secrets and strategies that human beings have a propensity to harbour. One is that they've an unmet need which a has delivered about them ache and could accomplish that for the rest of their lives. This can be a lack of interest or parental guide at key moments of their early life as

49

an example. Or possibly considered sincerely one in every of their dad and mom have come to be completely absent. Whatever it's miles, begin to play that function for them.

Two, they'll have fantasies or tendencies to act out which is probably frowned upon through wider society. If this is the case, provide them with a solid area to indulge in the ones impulses. These also are probable to originate from early life. Therefore, at the same time as the revelation of truth takes location, they may come to be childlike of their behaviour. This is the instant to capture control and manual them down the direction of 'lived fact' to complete the manipulation.

By giving them the opportunity to relive their burden and stay out their fantasies, you switch out to be impossible to resist to them.

Look for clues in their outward behaviour. Whatever trait they show off as a part of their man or woman, attention on what the alternative need to appear like. This is usually how these items pass.

The uptight generally have a tendency to crave adventure and relinquishing in their responsibilities. The adventurous can regularly be located secretly craving for the quiet existence and dream of everyday. Loud, brash human beings may be hiding insecurities approximately themselves. Quiet parents may be decided to discover the only who will offer them a platform to open up. They will be inclined to have the darkest secrets and techniques and techniques.

Appear Predictable, but be Far From it

The chaotic truth is not out of place on us however in place of take shipping of this, we earnestly plough on with our tries to preserve order. People crave form and familiarity to ease the innate anxiety that lurks internal them.

Our area in the universe is far from positive and this idea is by no means too some distance from the floor of human beings's fragile minds. Ease humans's fears thru presenting them with the familiarity they want to 'stay to tell the tale'.

Become a dependable buddy who may be called upon in instances of need. Be sincere for your call for and maintain forth a clean set of values to that you seemingly typically adhere to.

People are usually jogging highbrow simulations to artwork others out. This can be benevolent unconscious programming or a planned try and exercising session your actions.

Regardless of their intentions, you want to let them take shipping of as proper with they understand you internal out. Present yourself as a predicable person living a quite bland life.

When humans don't count on you to perform a little element out of the ordinary, they proper away start to underestimate you - imparting you with the top hand. You can take gain in their faux sense of superiority with the aid of secretly engaging in a deceptive marketing campaign inside the course of them.

If you are openly unpredictable you run the risk of intimidating humans. You will discover it difficult to attract humans close to you and your powers of manipulation is probably minimum. Only whilst you may effectively convince others of your predictability are you able to flow full throttle on your wildness.

Out of sight and out of mind, you can revenue your interest of manipulation via orchestrating a series of unexpected moves that reputedly pop out of left field. When your goal is aware about that something goes to expose up, however they don't recognize at the same time as, why and with the aid of who - they'll be capable of literally be driven to madness. Causing madness can also additionally also be a purpose in itself.

Use Your Words Sparingly

Talk in all fairness-priced. Words are all too common in our global of verbal diarrhoea and on-line narcissistic Tweet fuck monologues. In a world in which there is an abundance of voiced evaluations, you can mark yourself out as wonderful via manner of refusing to play ball. The greater you are pronouncing the more likely you're to say some issue stupid or to show your right intentions.

As human beings, we experience a deep revel in of urgency to recognize what the alternative man or woman thinks. We dive without delay into this relentless hobby thru the usage of asking probing questions while we enter a social situation.

By sparingly the use of your terms, you may manage a enjoy of effective mystique spherical you.

The less you supply in communique the more the alternative man or woman might be compelled to fill the regions with senseless babbling - as a way to growth the chances that they'll be people who show an excessive amount of approximately themselves.

Demonstrate your energy through your restraint and others round you could bend on the knee to blurt out statistics if you need to later be utilized in competition to them, via way of you.

Use Spies & Become a Spy

In your pursuit of absolute energy, there'll come a factor in which your personal talents are driven onto a restriction of kinds. You can't probably recognize the entirety but that shouldn't prevent you from challenge any choice which you secretly harbour - no matter out outlandish and grand it can seem.

If your venture of manipulation calls so one can walk into the lion's den, you want to use all assets available to you. When concentrated on a person of immoderate esteem, you may regularly want help. You should recruit spies who can inform you of your intention's recurring, pursuits, and peculiarities.

In the age of the internet, that is extra feasible because of humans's readiness to verbally defecate their each belief on blogs and social media. Yet the real records is probably determined offline - and that's why you need assist so that you can penetrate the picture that your goal has carefully cultivated for the relaxation of the world.

The reality is that there are various succesful manipulators who have possibly been gambling this game hundreds longer than you. When you decide to make a play for a throne by manner of the use of making considered one in each of them your goal, your non-public abilities might be tested in comparison to ever in advance than. Therefore, it's critical to no longer get complacent - you want to use a couple of belongings of statistics and be prepared to sabotage them on all fronts if required.

Other master manipulators will recognise no longer to allow humans in on their actual intentions. When you stumble upon them, you can by no means get a glimpse in their real feelings or critiques.

This level of opposing capability dictates that if you need to obtain fulfillment at the pinnacle echelons of the meals chain, you need to have a study what they do in region of what they're saying.

The use of spies is important for this task. What are they in fact doing with their time? Who do they liaise with? What are their obsessions and person defects? Are there additives in their normal that they appear too connected to? These are all perfect questions to are searching out answers to for your try and take the throne.

Pay spies if you need to. Do a few aspect it takes to get facts with out compromising your venture. After all, you don't want your intentions to be found out with the useful resource of a misstep that indicators them to the reality which you are coming for them.

Should your potential spies be too risky to hire due to reliability or ineptitude, play the function of secret agent yourself. This increases the time needed to take the throne as you are now playing a trustworthy longer sport. However, it's miles nonetheless viable this way.

In this situation you have to insert your self because the buddy, usually taking an hobby in their lives on the equal time as closing as quiet as possible approximately your very own.

During snug social occasions, possibilities normally arise so that it will get glimpses into the manner they quietly go with the flow approximately their commercial employer.

If you do this in an professional way, the usage of all of your guile and silent doggedness, you can stumble onto all their flaws one after the alternative through the years. Remember, this isn't the Spanish inquisition - it's a 'real' friendship you are providing wherein notable chatter is the order of the day.

Savvy operators are best probably to allow their shield down once they lighten up into as an alternative 'meaningless' verbal exchange. Gently guiding the conversation to emotional topics, together with arguable ones in the records, you open them as tons as them becoming emotional themselves after which mistakenly revealing a key piece of records that lets in you positioned their puzzle together.

Once you're in ownership of their 'reality', you're now prepared to take their throne for yourself.

Total Annihilation

When you effectively manage a person to scouse borrow their throne, you create a lifelong enemy. Nobody loves to be dethroned, lose social popularity or any shape of battle - specifically one that they had no idea they were preventing that changed into expertly completed by means of manner of a grasp manipulator such as you.

Once your tooth have sunk into your intention's jugular, there is no room for reprieve. Should you deliver in to any fleeting feeling of pity or sympathy that you can have, you risk dropping everything.

At this aspect in the game, the enemy in them has already been usual. You ought to give up the interest and dispose of all their receding strength, even if your victory has already been acquired.

This isn't always any time for mercy - show your fury and launch the rage that burns internal you.

Offer a New Cause to Maintain your Throne

The need and choice to control ought to no longer cease what you have got acquired a throne. No, this is wherein the work have to high-quality actually virtually start. Once you have got got finished a large personal victory like this, your devious self perception will rise to new, more risky ranges.

Your thirst for energy will swell, as will other people's perceptions of you. This is the super time to foster a cult-like feeling - with the top of the cult being you.

In a time on the equal time as religion is at the decline global, unorganised spirituality continues to proliferate. This is due to the fact humans are inclined and ever desperate to believe in a few aspect, a few issue.

They want a cause to champion, a divine being to worship and an purpose in their very very personal pitiful life. You need to be equipped to capture in this weird innate preference which drives the loads.

To control a cult like following of you, you have to capture the attention of these round you. Speak in grandiose terms, promising and detailing a more vision of the future. Wax lyrical approximately this utopia this is coming, specializing in how magical it's far going to be.

Keep it indistinct even though - don't overpromise on the particular records as so one can set you up for failure later on. Just interest on raising arousal in the crowd if you want to make their very private connections. Let them fill their non-public intellectual canvas and dream their non-public desires. They will then function credit score to you for the effective sensations stirring internal of them.

The reality is that most people's actual-existence troubles are complex, however they'll be all too glad to rally round a 'easy' answer if provided to them with favored self belief.

This is because the not unusual character has a terrifying mixture of incompetence and laziness which stops them from ever being the masters of their very own fate. They crave a draw close – will you be their saviour?

Eliminate boredom from turning into a ability trouble with the resource of terrific humans together together with your grandeur. This is the time so that you can step into the emperor's robes and to put on them with a ambitious smile for your face.

Give human beings a faux sense of repute through method of creating a fake hierarchy in which humans with higher accolades honestly begin to agree with they have got real strength. Let those decided on few bathe to your affirmation. They becomes your largest defenders further to being a beneficial guard as they end up targets of envy to those below them, who want 'electricity' for themselves. By permitting them to put on their non-public lesser metaphorical robes, they will be first in line to take a bullet need to matters get heated.

Once human beings acquire their region, the time is ripe to increase an us vs them narrative. Nothing unites a tough and speedy more than a common enemy. Fire up the self-righteousness in your lovers by way of manner of creating them virtuous and irritated!

Keep them triggered to live with you by means of repeatedly

highlighting the advantages of being in your unique following, similarly to ruthlessly demonstrating what takes region to outsiders. If there is no enemy on the way to rally against, simply invent one.

Master manipulators examine early immediately to openly observe traditions and traditional beliefs of the way of life. Being seen to be in the direction of generations of organisation wondering is a unstable workout. If you crave freedom, the high-quality way to collect it is through bland conformity. This might also furthermore appear counter-intuitive, however it permits you to be left by myself to play out your private mind, some distance from prying and dangerous interest.

Control their Perception

Perception is the crucial element to how we understand fact. By controlling the notion of the loads, you keep the keys to manipulating their minds. It is the remaining energy to be had to realize manipulators who are at the pinnacle in their sport.

Each one people is the unmarried component of hobby of an countless consciousness - however most people don't recognize this. You may not understand this, but it's miles the vital detail to know-how our proper powers. To enact this very last level of the game of manipulation you need to lessen human beings off from this truth.

Perception is everything.

People's behaviour is dictated totally via way of their belief of fact. Interpretation of facts results in a sure behaviour in response to that interpretation. Impose your very personal perception of truth thru manipulating the statistics that human beings gather. This is the manner to ensure a whole population can behave in a manner that fits you.

Therefore you need to censor the output of records so you can display you in a terrible mild or result in an immediate project to your authority. Spread rumours about your opponents and particular master manipulators who pose the most essential risk to you. Crush them in a maelstrom of faux statistics.

The secret is to dose human beings right into a trance, so that they live psychologically asleep. Give them addictive technology which they apparently select to feed their minds on - then use that generation to manipulate and pacify them.

Those who expect they're courageous and who get near the reality must be painted as 'loopy' and 'conspiracy theorists'. Nobody gets unnoticed more than the ones we accept as true with to have misplaced their minds.

Be positive to cultivate a way of life of 'political correctness' in which the grip on what human beings can and might't say is tightened. The an awful lot less free speech there may be, the simpler it is going to be to overwhelm dissent need to it rise up.

As this manner of existence evolves you will be able to do a remarkable deal much less artwork as human beings will 'self-police' out of worry - ultimately, it's top notch to understand some other character out to dry for their errors than they themselves come to be the person who is hanged.

Chapter 4: Explanation of the technological information and workout of hypnosis in notable element

In the hypnotic trance, the issue's thoughts is in a receptive condition, making it simple to implant new thoughts.

One ought to mention he has the capability to tap into the subconscious while however final absolutely aware.

Here, I'll break down the technological knowledge inside the again of hypnosis and percent some attempted-and-actual techniques for drifting off speedy and peacefully.

How exactly does hypnosis paintings?

As end up previously set up, hypnosis is characterized with the aid of a heightened receptivity to idea.

It retains its very very own sense of self-hobby even because it taps into the unconscious.

The potential to simply accept new information and to count on visually improves while one's normal nation of hobby is disrupted.

It's common for human beings to enjoy a heightened or distorted interest sometimes.

Hypnosis comes with out troubles to me at the same time as my thoughts is calm and focused.

While looking television, hypnosis is the most common nation.

The lifestyles of tv has prolonged been associated with self-guarantee and enjoyment.

It's the form of location in which all of us can benefit that trancelike frame of thoughts.

Furthermore, a few people are more open to hypnosis than others.

It's not clean to remove individuals who are inflexible of their ideals and values.

Someone who is scared of being hypnotized due to the fact they anticipate they may be not able to control their actions.

Many hypnotizable humans circulate into the experience with the concept that they want to restore a few difficulty, and that hypnosis is the manner to do it.

You can first-class feel compassion if you're in a place of receive as true with (a nation in that you open your coronary coronary coronary heart to the opportunity person and feature goodwill).

It is a great deal much less hard to enter a hypnotic u.S..

In its most critical shape, Lapole is created between humans whilst they're in touch with every different, once they trust every distinctive, and when they find spending time together fun.

There is a propensity for the thoughts to enter a trance-like situation referred to as the Lapole country.

Alters one's united states of popularity to rewrite one's unconscious with tips and analogies (parables).

One of the maximum common uses of hypnosis is to regulate a person's worldview (unconscious).

Similar to how all of us has encountered stereotypical portrayals, clearly all and sundry has encountered ideals.

Although this is an inherent human technique, it has been technologically harnessed inside the exercising of hypnosis.

Tips on Inducing Hypnosis

If you need to be hypnotized, you need to comply with this sequence.

A. Hypnosis's Growing Popularity

Two, assemble a truthful connection (promise safety and protection).

Induce hypnosis, then make suggestions.

Hypnotic Regression 4

It is essential that you stay with this right technique.

Engaging with hypnosis with an open thoughts and a willingness to bear in mind in it is a important step.

Advice and techniques that may be utilized in enterprise and love

People's first mind, I remember, are of hypnosis shows and acts on TV when they pay attention the phrase.

For some, this may conjure pics of occult or psychic competencies.

Some can also additionally moreover surprise, "Isn't it Yarase?" or "Isn't it required to have a special electricity?"

However, hypnosis can be idea of as a sort of intellectual generation.

Treated as hypnosis, self-hypnosis and university problem, hypnosis is employed in the direction of our lives.

The functionality to mesmerize on purpose may be found out by manner of every person with understanding of the underlying mechanisms and sure realistic tips.

Examine the following claims and determine in the occasion that they follow to you:

The human mind fascinates me, and I would like to beautify my communique abilties and conversational directing abilities in order that I can:

If you revel in this manner, gaining knowledge of approximately hypnosis can be of super use to you.

If the mission does no longer observe be hypnotized, then you definitely definately cannot hypnotize them. It's clean that many humans may additionally furthermore have a defective data of hypnosis.

So, allow me fill you in on the fundamentals of hypnosis so that you can begin the use of it efficiently right away. Many of these principles have previously been delivered; however, as I said at the ebook's outset, it is critical to take a look at the requirements regularly so you can make sure that your subconscious absolutely is acquainted with and makes use of them:

Hypnosis, as you apprehend, entails manipulating every other person's mind and body via "strategies that make you believe you studied."

To intricate a piece, below hypnosis, information is stored within the subconscious mind each time the hassle concentrates on a wonderful difficulty bear in mind.

Feelings of unconsciousness are more not unusual than the ones of consciousness.

"Iconic lemon check."

Think of a lemon you are maintaining for your proper hand. Think of the lemon on your head as in reality as possible. It has an ethereal, blue fragrance and a slightly gritty texture.

The lemon has a notch, so lessen it in half of. The juice must seep out of the middle and feature a pleasant, energizing heady scent. Enjoy a smooth lemon chunk.

You can taste the lemon and sense its sourness at some point of your tongue. Did you be aware a present day launch of saliva?

When you consciousness your interest more, you may study that more saliva flows out of your mouth.

In fact, it's far hypnosis as well.

People's imagination (picture location) is especially robust.

In the equal way that the mere intellectual conjuring of a lemon reasons an increase in saliva manufacturing, the mere highbrow conjuring of any object can create physiological changes in someone or girls. That's the essence of hypnosis.

2. The Impact of Hypnosis

By the manner, if you rent this "hypnosis" efficaciously, you could expect various outcomes. Hypnosis end up at the start practiced as a manner to calm stressful thoughts.

Hence, it has the ability to prompt a kingdom of calm.

Hypnosis is a country in which attention is installation at the intermediate fee amongst sleep and wakefulness.

Creating this sort of nation calls for hundreds of labor and workout, but it is not hard to get it to the issue wherein it seems like a dream.

When in this circumstance, it's miles tough for power to go into the frame, necessitating: • strain reduce price • a shift towards a more high-quality worldview.

• Overcoming shortcomings, and so on.

The final results is to be expected. The premise of each yoga and meditation are comparable.

Hypnosis is a way to lighten up each bodily and mentally, make bigger your thoughts and launch yourself from pressure. You'll begin feeling higher nearly right away, and you could make huge improvement in the direction of your desires.

Instances one thru 3 wherein hypnosis is useful

We can truly absolutely everyone benefit from hypnosis if we discover ways to use it well.

In this context, "way of life enhancement" may also mean a few aspect from "recalling antique memories" to "handling ache" to "overcoming assets you are not precise at" to "digital sports activities experience" to "a a fulfillment weight loss program," and so forth.

Hypnosis is commonly used to address parents with psychosomatic illnesses, depression, and exclusive intellectual problems inside the United States, a superior u . S . A . In the use of hypnosis.

Of route, it is carried out with the beneficial useful resource of a informed therapist who has mastered scientific hypnosis strategies, counseling capabilities, medical statistics, and so on.

Practical programs of hypnosis.

When seen as a branch of psychology, hypnosis has surprising packages outdoor of clinical settings.

The well-known "suspension bridge effect" amongst humans is a form of self-hypnosis.

Other techniques encompass "mirroring," which creates a experience of familiarity with the resource of mimicking the opportunity character's movements and sporting events, and "double bind," which makes it extra convenient to in fact take transport of the YES of the opportunity party thru giving them alternatives. Therefore, in our every day life, hypnosis is hired anywhere.

The goal market for your lectures, suggests, and romantic endeavors will understand your interest in intellectual techniques, mainly replicate strategies that convey you toward the opportunity character. How can we appreciably enhance our verbal exchange capabilities thru the software of metaphor, the rhythm of the set of practices? Plus, take some time to share for your schooling.

Hypnosis: How to Use It, Part 2: Getting Ready

Now that you apprehend the basics of hypnosis, you may located your statistics to use.

But maximum of the time, hypnosis does not work if you try it on someone .

Preparation is the vital thing to a a hit hypnosis consultation, as with some other hobby. Let's discover what steps need to be taken earlier to supply the preferred final results.

Split into businesses, individuals who are and aren't without problems hypnotized.

Individual reaction to hypnosis varies dramatically. Those who're definitely receptive to hypnosis might be easily hypnotized with the aid of manner of honestly every body, whilst people who are evidence against hypnosis will stay resistant regardless of the capability of the hypnotist.

So, what distinguishes those who are much more likely to succumb to hypnosis from individuals who aren't?

People vulnerable to hypnosis.

People who are overly reliant on others

While under the impact of hypnosis, the affected man or woman will submit manage of his frame and mind to the hypnotist.

For this cause, it's miles hypothesized that social dependents and people with a immoderate diploma of social dependence are extra willing to take part. When comparing sexes, it appears that evidently ladies are more resultseasily hypnotized than adult men. As an aside, the foregoing is also the meant motive why hypnosis is difficult to use amongst human beings of the equal intercourse.

[2] Those who're progressive geniuses

The factor, whether or not or now not or now not with the useful resource of the usage of hypnosis converting one's feel of taste or thru hypnosis generating hallucinations, is how real and exquisite the resulting mental photo is.

Deep hypnotic software program is feasible via optimally utilizing the hypnotic aspect's effective images.

[3] Those with company convictions

Those who've a "love inside the starting sight" or "that is it" response also are liable to hypnosis.

Because it's miles clean to offer in to the hypnotist's pointers.

People that get more delight out of ordinary responsibilities are [4].

Those who are vulnerable to hypnosis are those who've the functionality to cognizance their hobby on a unmarried task.

It isn't a focus that starts offevolved the assessment with various statistics flowing in my thoughts, together with what is within the the front of me, the events surrounding me and guessing what is going to appear within the destiny.

Hypnosis needs attention that doesn't permit you to get into confusion thru observing most effective one factor or repeating an motion.

[5] Those which is probably able to precise their emotions certainly

When your feelings are at the surface, you're at risk of the ideas and moves of others round you.

"Funny and laughing," "I like what you do now not like," and "sad and impossible to resist" are just a few of the numerous hypnotic dominant feelings.

Those who have sturdy feelings are greater vulnerable to this hypnosis.

Invulnerable to hypnosis individuals

One who's suspicious approximately hypnosis

People who have a preexisting skepticism of hypnosis are notoriously difficult to hypnotize.

High-tension humans

Hypnosis is effective as it takes location subconsciously, but worry stands inside the way and motives a unconscious rejection of the hypnotic usa.

[3] The Ill

One needs to be as a minimum quite comfy to benefit from hypnosis.

Not being able to understand the hypnotist's instructions is a not unusual side effect of not getting sufficient rest or feeling well. It's possible that your muscle agencies are too tight to genuinely unwind.

Therefore, one's bodily fitness has a massive impact at the hypnotic nation.

Overly-tremendous people (4th)

There is a discrepancy between the actual hypnotic effect and the imagined hypnotic impact, giving the impact which you are not hypnotic even in case you are successful.

How to Get Ready for Hypnosis (Section 2-2)

Positivity is a vital issue in the hypnotic recipe for fulfillment.

Because hypnosis employs the approach of subconsciously influencing the target, it too is prone to abuse. This, however, is exactly off-limits.

Feeling like you are "thinking about the possibility character in a nice way" is a sense you have to in no manner forget about.

I supposed to buy a vacuum cleanser, so I went to an electronics shop, however the income partner become greater interested by selling the fridge. I doubt I'd purchase a vacuum from this kind of salesperson.

Rather, you'll possibly even experience enraged.

If "considering the alternative person in a pleasing way" is a essential tenet of your workout, you could no longer waste intellectual energy demanding approximately "what to do if hypnosis fails." Guide an exclusive sample if this one does not art work.

Thirdly, Hypnosis in Practice: How to Use It

Let's begin reading hypnosis right away.

As changed into formerly stated, hypnosis may be concept of as a highbrow "approach." Thus, it's miles essential which you perform the crucial strategies in the best order.

If I rely to three, my palms might not come off," you may see them show on TV.

The word "hypnosis" can also moreover make it seem as even though the approach is computerized, but in reality, hypnosis is usually caused through a series of steps taken by means of manner of the issue in advance than to the start of any transmission.

In different phrases, it is not feasible to skip all at once from the 0 situation to the hypnotic country. The accurate interpretation of hypnosis ought to be discovered.

Proposition three-1: Seek consent from the hypnotized man or woman.

Having the alternative man or woman take a look at be hypnotized is a critical first step.

Set the diploma for hypnosis (Step three-2)

The first-rate placing is a room that isn't always too mild, with an splendid temperature, a quiet and enclosed region for two human beings by myself.

Hypnosis does not comply with in careworn places. Find someplace quiet and out of the way wherein you could unwind.

In addition, human beings who can be hypnotized can be dominated via the hypnotist, consequently establishing an environment in which the issue can feel at peace will make it easier to be hypnotized.

Make certain there may be a comfortable couch or chair and that there may be no outside noise via the usage of turning off as many lights as you could.

Talk truely in advance than inducing hypnosis, as Step 3-three advises.

The hypnotic approach is implemented as a way to an surrender, however the onus is on the character to discover and address the issue(s) that inspire the favored exchange.

So, allow's have a serious speak about it. This will help you extend greater bear in mind with the hassle and benefit perception into the difficulty they may be coping with.

Drop the pitch of your voice and preserve a low tone as you speak. Nonetheless, you have to moreover be cognizant of the info of the tale you're telling.

This communicate, which takes region earlier than hypnosis, is essential. How you respond here will enormously decide your admittance into the following hypnosis.

three. Get in sync with the alternative character, after which 4. Get in even more sync with the opportunity individual.

Our next step may be to go into a rustic of profound hypnosis. Do no longer interrupt the go with the flow thru asserting, "Now I am going to hypnotize."

The goal of pre-hypnosis is to smooth the transition into whole hypnosis. Think of hypnosis as beginning the on the spot you input the hypnosis room. If you're synced, it will likely be clean to supply the "Please hypnotize" sign.

In one-of-a-kind terms, it induces hypnosis and synchronization inside the extraordinary person. And, through syncing with the opportunity party, the other facet may even synchronize unconsciously.

Do now not deny the affected character's information, but at the identical time as setting forward it, gently supply the character into profound hypnosis.

three-5. Adapt to the project's reply

If the individual reveals any physical or intellectual response, it must not be disregarded.

If he says some aspect like, "I'm sleepy" or "I'm heavy," we're capable of beef up the sensation with the resource of announcing a few aspect like, "And now you're even sleepier."

The frame earnings weight and weight and weight

Change our technique primarily based mostly on how the concern responds.

The aim is to preserve a consistent pace and tone inside the route of, without emphasizing any particular phrases. If the situation's reaction turns into even greater profound because of this, then the hypnosis can be very close to being a hit.

3-6. Awakening from hypnosis

After hypnotizing and running to cope with the problem, the priority ought to be woken (waking from hypnosis) (awakening from hypnosis).

Keep counting till you achieve some of that allows you to rouse frivolously and with out tension.

The unique birthday celebration also can dispute the efficacy of the hypnosis or expect the hypnotist modified into mendacity if the hypnosis finishes without awakening the affected person.

The extraordinary person's susceptibility to hypnosis will thereafter decrease.

Hypnosis's Four Uses

The utility of hypnosis can also deliver amazing blessings in every day life. Here, I'd want to provide an outline of hypnosis's potential uses.

Use in Business four-1

How familiar are you with the concept of rhythm? It isn't any exaggeration to nation that rhythm serves as a shape of hypnosis in addition to being a communication device.

Applying this approach within the profits corporation seems to be a surefire way to succeed. The earnings rhythm that might be achieved is as follows, so let's have a look at it.

Greeting each specific and commencing on foot

There remains a ways among the customer and the sale whilst you initially communicate with them.

This way that there can be presently no installed degree of be given as authentic with among the two activities. It's a tremendous day, so I'll greet you with some element like, "Hello."

By giving the client and the seller some difficulty in commonplace, this permits verbal exchange and breaks down obstacles. As brief as that wall vanishes, allow's skip lower lower back to industrial company.

Keeping up with the hints of your customers

Say, for argument's sake, that you private a residential business company.

Only some of clients are willing to give it a strive. They may also reject it, say it's miles high-priced or condemn the belongings itself.

In that proper away, "Neither the item nor the want of purchasing a home are cheap. Being slow is ideally suited, "Said pacing.

Imagine this as laying the basis for a sincere partnership on the side of your shoppers.

4-2. Apply to copywriting

It is recommended that, while using hypnosis to make a suggestion to another man or woman, you repeat the idea to further set off a trance inside the motive. Let's attempt it out in some sentence introduction!

Casually reiterating a product's promoting pitch is a first-rate method in case you discover one.

Perfect for use in advertising reproduction

The double bind works on the idea of presenting the caller with the records they may be looking for as if it had been already installed, and then switching gears to ask a one-of-a-kind inquiry.

For instance, assume you've got got text to sell beer that declares, "It's a excellent drink, each chilled or at room temperature."

This method assumes that customers will simply "drink (buy) beer" in place of weighing their alternatives and figuring out whether or no longer to make a buy.

Five Methods of Self-Hypnosis

Hypnotizing oneself (or self-hypnosis). Depending at the method, hypnosis could have profound results.

The electricity of concept is extraordinary; if you believe that some thing is warm sufficient to burn you, despite the truth that it is not, you may revel in the ache.

The benefits of self-hypnosis are severa, but handiest if you apprehend the manner to use it properly and located inside the time to workout it.

Here, I will in short describe a manner to exercise self-hypnosis.

Self-Hypnosis Preparation 5-1

First, find out a secluded spot.

It's critical to exercising self-hypnosis somewhere personal and non violent.

In addition, it's miles important to do away with all anxieties. Take into attention your personal non-public priorities, together with how sticky you are, how an entire lot time you need to get organized, and what you have were given planned for tomorrow.

To take the second one step, format a tranquil surroundings.

Next, placed on light, acquainted apparel to generate a snug nation. Fabrics that make you experience bulky or weighed down should be prevented.

Afterward, pass unwind somewhere snug. Those who're capable of unwind on a bed or blanket may also find out a sofa or chair to be a welcoming place to rest their our bodies and minds.

Third, make it pitch black in there.

Also, try to get as plenty darkness as you could in right proper here. It's handiest to set it to a relaxing installing choice to clearly turning it off.

Before diving headfirst into self-hypnosis, it could be beneficial to visualize the very last results you are after. As you close up up your eyes, think as especially as you may.

Self-hypnosis on the time great worried a single belief. You won't be able to patiently look beforehand to the impact if there are too many.

You can use a pendulum or a metronome to set up a ordinary beat even as you're organized to move that a ways.

Using Hypnosis on Oneself (Stage 5-2)

Once you have got got had been given the rhythmic device, you can relax and recognition your hobby.

Keep staring till you could no longer make out whatever however the rhythm gadgets in the room. Close your eyes progressively when you're capable of reputation at the rhythm gadgets.

Following that, I became preoccupied with unfocused mind of my destiny self, my aspirations, and my modern-day degree of success.

The idea isn't to assume forcefully, however alternatively to expect only visually. Consider the photograph as a few aspect that exists in its herbal country.

fifty threeGetting Ready for Bed

If the entirety is going effortlessly and the photo is high-quality enough, you may find your self turning into sleepy.

Then, permit's supply in to our exhaustion and go to sleep. Say some component like, "When you wake up, you may enjoy cushty sleeping and spell binding," right earlier than you go with the flow off to sleep.

If you're capable of doze off and wake up without any trouble, self-hypnosis has been a achievement.

By again and again education this, you need to bring about hypnosis in yourself. It's vital to no longer take away doing this due to the reality you bear in mind the bar is just too excessive.

You can use the time before mattress, and the lack of guidance will help you loosen up and focus extra deeply.

Seventh Synopsis Although the time period "hypnosis" may additionally conjure pictures of a mysterious workout, it's miles genuinely pretty commonplace and has many applications out of doors of the vicinity of psychotherapy.

The maximum essential subjects are being nicely-prepared and having a dependable rapport with the issue.

Hypnosis is a few component you must try, as it will will let you and the humans spherical you.

How to use hypnosis for the number one time

As we've already mentioned, hypnosis is a very commonplace phenomenon that all and sundry experience generally in our daily lives.

Hypnosis is a circumstance close to sleep.

Everything about contemporary-day existence is hypnotic, from morning awakenings to binge-watching tv after some beverages.

Hypnotizing human beings is simple.

Many dad and mom may additionally have a suspicious picture almost about hypnosis.

But hypnosis is an technique that uses psychology to accumulate its desires.

It is researched as a area of study in Japanese universities and is practiced as a remedy in Europe and the us. A greater acceptable lifestyles is promised to individuals who devote themselves to reading and training effective hypnosis.

Anyone can utilize hypnosis as long as they've got mastered it.

Here, consequently, are the nine measures I recommend taking in advance than trying hypnosis for the number one time.

Mastering hypnosis is useful in masses of contexts; you may positioned your newfound talents to apply for your expert existence, romantic relationships, and further.

Get the alternative character's permission earlier than hypnotizing them.

This is an crucial assumption for mastering to hypnotize.

Do no longer attempt to hypnotize the man or woman you are rejecting, however paintings with the man or woman's information and cooperation.

Foresight in the shape of a proposal earlier than hypnosis

Suggestion is on the coronary coronary heart of hypnosis.

Make a statement that informs you in reality what to do with hypnosis.

Be exceptional to prepare a recommendation in advance and memorize it firmly.

For perfect hypnotic results, put together your self earlier.

An person's receptivity to hypnosis can be determined with the assist of a proposal test.

Inducing hypnosis sEnter hypnosis as an introduction to hypnosis.

To collect a more profound hypnotic trance, the deepening method is usually recommended.

You can greater reliably induce hypnosis for your hands by using way of manner of telling your self things like, "Your right arm will loosen up and relax," or a few tremendous similar phrase.

offers a cause for hypnosis

You can also additionally strive counting to three and growing a noise, like snapping your fingers or clapping your palms, in case you've ever seen a hypnosis software program.

Consistency in stimuli will growth their effectiveness.

A Hypnotic State

That's the dominion the concept depicts.

It is essential at this diploma that the opposite aspect has a complete hold close of the situation.

If you supply in to the hypnotist's tips, you open your self as tons as greater manipulation.

Make an attempt to make movement and feeling suggestions that predominate.

Hypnosis, regularly located in hypnosis indicates, wherein the frame does not waft or the body collapses whilst fame, is named exercising manipulate and the exchange in flavor is known as sensory manage.

It's the foundation of hypnosis workout and the manner it's far used.

Make a proposal that you would love to actually be given, if viable.

Once your motor and sensory mastery is finished and you're extra prone to hypnosis, supply your self a few thoughts.

Naturally, it can first embody workout or sensory mastery till you switch out to be acquainted with hypnosis.

Instruct to cancel the inspiration

If you're willing to famend that you had been hypnotized, the hypnosis session may be terminated.

Simply

After three blows of your finger, all your guidelines may be nullified and you may be invited again.

Remember that it handiest takes a touch to suggest that.

Over time, hypnosis can fade away, even without explicit instructions to interrupt the trance.

Resolving the approach without letting skip of the scenario will make it look like the hypnotherapist have turn out to be wrong and could purpose the problem to lose religion in hypnosis. In that example, it will in all likelihood be hard to apply the approach the following time.

"Even after the hypnosis is ended, if I provide him the equal idea, he may be hypnotized again," you will inform your self in advance than trying to hypnotize the identical man or woman over again.

Well stated.

Also, the secretary can get the incorrect idea and expect she's in spite of the reality that underneath hypnosis in case you do now not cancel the concept.

Be positive to dispose of the idea at the prevent of the hypnosis.

Summary

Many human beings might imagine that hypnosis is quite difficult and takes a few precise facts.

However, as I set up in this talk, hypnosis can be utilized by everybody.

Practice is the great way to boom one's hypnotic capabilities. No you will be able to get it right from the start.

Once you have mastered the art work of hypnotism, it may open up an entire new global of possibilities for you.

Chapter 5: Dave Elman Induction

An Altered Induction thru the usage of Dave Elman

American hypnotist Dave Elman pioneered this method for producing a hypnotic usa. As a end end result of its fast induction and deepening of hypnosis and its reliability in gauging responsiveness, it has become more and more famous amongst cutting-edge hypnotherapists. The technique typically consists of the subsequent degrees, which may be separated thru using recommendations for greater in-depth relaxation at each degree:

1. Relax by way of remaining your eyes and breathing deeply.

The Persuader of Excessive Arm Weight (decrease arm to check and suggest muscle relaxation).

A Convincing Method for Ocular Catastrophic Epilepsy (notion that the problem cannot open his eyes).

Third, recurrent eye closure can similarly set off hypnosis (repeated reinduction) 4. "Losing the numbers", deepening for intellectual relaxation and amnesia test.

In an elevator, a deepener is a device used to make the automobile deeper (optionally to be had).

A series of (convincing) tests and deepenings that Elman appears to have commonly done following a watch fixation induction or certainly after inquiring for the patient to close his eyes are typically known as the "Elman induction," irrespective of the fact that this isn't always what Elman in reality did.

The whole induction method often takes no extra than 3 to five minutes. It's possibly that the purchaser's full-size boom in suggestibility throughout those three minutes is because of the short modifications and critiques the patron undergoes in the direction of that point. It is instructive to evaluation this method with the quite commonplace 10-15 minute "cutting-edge relaxation induction" often used by many hypnotherapists.

There is a wonderful mixture of physical concept (losing the arm to mean rest of tensions and letting pass, time and again starting and last the eyes) and the splendid use of task checks (also referred to as "convincers"): now not being capable of open the eyelids. The "not having the potential to mention the numbers" is used with a lively fluidity that induces hypnosis unexpectedly (and conforms to your preconceived notions of what hypnosis is like: a surreal revel in at some point of which you are not capable of open your eyes or utter your private call).

Take our Certificate course in evidence-primarily based totally hypnosis or our Diploma in Cognitive Behavioral Hypnotherapy to discover about Elman induction, eyelid closure induction, arm levitation induction, script writing, deepeners, ache manipulate, self-hypnosis, and masses more.

Personal transcribing thru Elman

Here, in his very very very own phrases, is Elman's renowned induction device, taken immediately from his 1964 e-book, Hypnotherapy.

Immediately Initiating

"Would you thoughts taking some moments to loosen up and close to your eyes?" Now loosen up the muscle agencies round your eyes to the thing in which those eye muscle groups won't perform and while you're confident they may no longer art work, attempt them and make certain they might not paintings.... [Subject rubs sleep from his eyes.] In truth, with the aid of making sure their functionality, you're making sure their fulfillment. Let your guard all of the way right all the way down to the component in that you understand they will now not paintings, and then, when you're remarkable, supply them a strive. Try them tough. Spend some fantastic downtime letting your ocular muscle groups unwind.... [Client is now exhibiting catalepsy in the eyelids.] Now, permit that experience of ease attain all of the way right all the way down to your toes.... In a second, we are going to try this all over again, and the second time round, you'll be capable of rest even more deeply than you've got up to now.

Open your eyes. Just shut your eyes. Let all your problems melt away and lighten up your body and thoughts. Now the zero.33 time we do that you could double the rest you've got. To unwind, open your eyes. If you have been following the commands to this point, your hand ought to fall limp into your lap as I launch it from my draw near. Please wait till I enhance it, no. That's notable in case you pull it up and make it heavy, but now allow's open and close our eyes all yet again, doubling the soothing outcomes and sending them all the way right down to our toes. May the burden of that hand be as crushing as lead.... When you eventually discover authentic relaxation, you could apprehend it. You have it now. Maybe you had a experience of that. (Cause of lack of life: positive, affected person) " Delving Even Further " That's a rustic of entire physical rest, however I moreover want to expose you the manner to unwind mentally, so once I say, begin counting backwards from 100. Double your kingdom of rest whenever I say quite diverse, and by the point I acquire 98, you will be so cushty that you may not even be aware. Put in movement the belief of creating it arise, and you'll see it materialize. Please remember aloud. A hundred (Patient) Increase your country of calmness, and the disappearing digits will accelerate. (Ninety-nine.) See the figures start to vanish in advance than your eyes. (Ninety-8.) Now they will be long gone.... Make it arise. You want to do it because of the reality I may not. Make them vanish, fall apart them, erase them. Have we misplaced them all? [The subject initially answers "yes," but after Elman questions and tests him, he realizes the subject is "too exhausted to continue."]

Get rid of the figures altogether, please. Expel them... Is that the case? Disappear them, please. You'll improve your hand, and when I drop it, all the ones distinct digits will vanish. Do you choice for them to pull decrease again and stand through the use of as you... Is that the case? (Yes.)" Elman, Hypnotherapy (1964), pp. 60–sixty 5.

"Just lighten up," starts the altered version of Elman's creation script. Put your arms for your lap or rest them at the desk.

Now gaze up and reduce again as in case you have been trying to reputation on a place to your forehead at the equal time as bending your head ahead slightly. That's pushing it, however you need to persist. While retaining this upward and backward gaze, inhale deeply till your lungs are sincerely whole. Just a sec at the equal time as we pause. As you slowly and patiently exhale, hold your gaze consistent upward and your eyes closed. Now, all systems skip, relax from your head in your feet. Relax like a rag doll and allow your muscle groups loosen up and sag.

Now, rest your attention on the ones eyelids all yet again. Even in case your eyes have already closed, photo them doing so once more, this time feeling even more dreary, sleepy, and sluggish than they did the primary time. Close your eyes so gently that it seems like they may not open yet again. Once you have got were given finished that, you may check to appearance within the event that they sincerely revel in like they are sealing. Push more difficult toward that relaxation and realize that the extra you try to make the effort, the extra sluggish, torpid and cushty those eyelids have end up in the meanwhile. Put an surrender to your efforts and loosen up the part of you that have become straining to accomplish that. Your eyelids aren't sincerely sealed, it most effective looks as if they will be. The truth that you can allow you to realize are honestly unwinding is encouraging.

Here, I'll show you a manner to in addition deepen your u . S . Of relaxation. In a minute I will depend #1, 2, 3, once I get to quantity three you can open your eyes for a second in advance than you gesture and utter the word "sleep". Upon invoking the command "sleep," all you need to do is near your eyes and you may discover your self once more in hypnosis, handiest greater so than earlier than. Now, one, , 3... Close your eyes, get prepared for "sleep," and take a miles longer, more profound nap than regular. Again, rely to 3, close your eyes, and say "sleep"; this time, permit yourself bypass two times as deeply. Now, one, , 3, open your eyes enormous, get organized to "sleep," and lighten up even greater deeply than before.

Now you're exciting the frame very profoundly, and as you loosen up the frame you're enjoyable the thoughts. I'm going to reveal you the way to calm your mind even further proper now. In a minute, I want you to begin counting backwards from 100. It will simplest take some digits, and whilst you rely, you have to grade by grade decrease your voice till you're counting in a whisper and in the end in silence, due to the fact the hypnotherapist is presently doing to demonstrate.

Over time, at the same time as the voice calms down, the numbers gets more difficult and more hard to make out.

Whisper the number one range, then be silent as you count it to yourself. Just start counting, and as you do, allow your mind wander and your muscle corporations loosen up.

[Exchange recommendations to relax voice and fade into quiet until subject stops counting].

Yes, this is the entirety. Good. Now unwind even in addition, and at the same time as you are at it, deliver it your all to bear in mind the ones phone numbers, most effective to discover that you can not discover them anywhere."

Chapter 6: What occurs in the thoughts?

Hypnosis as a topic of check.

If you pay attention closely, you can pick out out out the phrases "makes you sleepy" due to the fact the pendulum swings backward and forward. Moreover, the moment your finger touches... Like hypnosis like this has been seen through all of us. Hypnosis is not simplest a trick, regardless of what many might also bear in thoughts. That hypnosis is viable and can produce observable neural changes is supported through research. As a shape of remedy, it is endorsed by way of some psychologists a terrific way to enhance sufferers' physiological and intellectual nicely-being. Observations of humans's thoughts waves have shed slight at the diverse susceptibilities of various human beings to hypnosis. Video from YouTube's "scishow" channel, a fave amongst scientific buffs, presenting the test of hypnosis.

Hypnosis is not some type of con

The Reverend Michael Aranda: Your interest will go with the flow off to dreamland in case you stare at a pendulum-swinging clock all night time time. In addition, the complete clip will play as short as you contact the display.

There isn't any doubt which you have witnessed hypnosis like this. As within the movie "Office Space," issuing orders, shrieking like a duck, and even switching personas. Skeptics have doubts approximately this hypnosis because of the manner it appears to artwork. Maybe this watch and this voice are more potent than I apprehend, but I doubt it.

As an extended manner as I can tell, hypnosis is not some thing you pull out for some laughs at a celebration. Scientific studies have confirmed that hypnosis is viable and can produce great neural changes. Psychologists can also propose it as a recovery method for boosting every your physical and intellectual health.

121

In that case, hypnosis may be actual. The capability for indoctrination isn't always exaggerated. Trance studies and diverse sorts of meditation had been defined for thousands of years.

Modern hypnosis is regularly credited to a scientific doctor named Franz Mesmer, who labored inside the 1700s.

The historical figure who gave upward push to the word "hypnotize." Mezmer proposed an reason of the natural international that he dubbed "animal magnetism." Clearly, there was extra happening than smooth sexual attraction.

In his thoughts, all living matters have been permeated with the resource of an unseen current of magnetic stress. He claimed that with the resource of manipulating the float, any infection may be remedied.

With low lighting, enigmatic tune, magnetic forces, and a sequence of gestural turns on, he tried to keep the affected person out of his trance and restore equilibrium to the invisible flow. In the wake of that, some formerly ill humans recovered.

The chemical network, after analyzing the animals' magnetic forces, got here to the belief that the go with the glide of magnetic pressure did now not correlate with progressed recovery abilities. Mezmer's research are not taken severely, and trans remedy has ceased to be a feasible possibility for scientific improvement.

However, scientific professional James Blade started looking at this treatment possibility in the center of the 1800s.

The term "hypnosis," derived from the Greek phrase "hypnos" and given to me for explanation features, is my invention. Since being in a trance felt very just like being asleep.

Hypnosis is generally associated with sleepiness inside the minds of present day medical psychologists. Hypnotic consciousness is a lot like meditating. Unlike the showy hypnosis on television, scientific hypnosis is in particular smooth. Concentration, it clearly is all.

Subtle tunes play in the history, however clearing the course is the number one aim. The hypnotist speaks softly and encourages the affected man or woman to pay interest, like with a pocket watch that periodically shakes. Allow them a few down time, too. As a end result, they'll be much less guarded and further receptive to your recommendation. Depending on the desired effects of hypnosis, the hypnotherapist can also direct the affected individual to peer high-quality situations or supply particular commands. Simple, isn't it?

Characteristics of hypnotizable and nonhypnotizable human beings that make the previous greater vulnerable to its have an effect on

Clinical psychologists generally agree that hypnosis dreams to spark off a deep nation of relaxation and popularity. Hypnosis has competing intellectual factors.

The altered kingdom of interest is whilst hypnosis leads to a few other recognition. It's a fantastic highbrow state altogether, analogous to sleep, in which typical perception strategies are altered or possibly absent.

Non-kingdom precept, as an alternative, compares hypnosis to acting in a play.

It's no longer a chemical or physical exchange within the mind like an altered state of attention; as an alternative, it is the cease end end result of focused hobby and the hypnotic power of concept. In a nutshell, you're conscious and you are not breaking any crook recommendations. Additionally, researchers now require extra evidence to psychologically make clean hypnosis.

Some human beings are more open to hypnosis than others, and that is widely recognized. The kingdom of hypnosis is selected with the resource of way of the character. You need to concentrate to the health practitioner, pay attention and try and lighten up.

Ten percent to fifteen percent of the populace can be especially open to hypnosis, consistent with research. These human beings are susceptible to hypnosis at some point of the session. Twenty percent of human beings are particularly evidence toward hypnosis. Others are combined.

It's unsure why he's so results hypnotized, even though dissecting his mind has discovered a diffused trade that probable performs a role.

The researchers used magnetic resonance imaging, or MRI.

According to the findings, the top of the corpus callosum grow to be extensively massive in those who were extra prone to hypnosis. That is the difficulty that controls hobby.

Other researchers have analyzed the thoughts waves of hypnotized sufferers. The mind, in a nutshell, cannot characteristic without a steady deliver of electrochemical energy. Why? Because nerves depend on it for communique.

Using EEG and EEG, the researchers tracked the work of the mind and determined various EEG patterns.

Studies have indicated that folks vulnerable to hypnosis are in particular susceptible to advanced theta waves. It has to do with interest and visualization. This is the state of affairs at the identical time as you are indulging in intellectual arithmetic or daydreaming.

Then, imaging techniques like magnetic resonance imaging and electroencephalography (EEG) located out the hypnotic united states's consequences on the brain's reputation. It lends credence to the idea of mellow cognizance.

Why is it left to the discretion of the hypnotist?

However, why does the affected person's outlook shift after being attentive to the scientific physician's recommendation?

It consists of the precept of top-down processing.

Input from the senses floods the thoughts. Having processed and interpreted the data, we've got were given were given a keep close to of the state of affairs. Therefore, in pinnacle-down processing, the facts saved in prolonged-term reminiscence and the expectancies usual thru inference have an impact on the records that is sensed and obtained at a decrease diploma.

This become commonplace facts amongst cognitive scientists. There are also various trials to examine this impact. People consume wine as it's to be had at lots of price elements. The wines I eat are the identical, however the wines which is probably considered luxurious are a touch tastier. Probably because I expected it to be delicious. More specially, the vicinity of the mind liable for happiness has prolonged in hobby.

The pinnacle-down method moreover describes the placebo effect. If you are taking a medicine that your scientific doctor thinks will enhance, you can discover it powerful. Yes, although it is handiest sugar.

Simply positioned, underneath hypnosis, human beings are greater receptive to new thoughts, and are greater willing to regulate their perspectives and expectancies for this reason. This hypnotic impact has additionally been examined experimentally.

The Stroop test is one such instance. Numerous terms exist to describe primary sunglasses like purple and blue. But in area of studying a phrase, it reads the color related to that word. There should be no yellow in a blue textual content.

That's a genuinely hard hassle to remedy. This is due to the fact the processing of phrases and phrase shades takes place simultaneously. The Stroop check became utilized by a fixed of neuroscientists to have a look at the outcomes of hypnosis. With the help of useful magnetic resonance imaging (fMRI), they appeared into the possibility of recording the colours associated with terms.

Both human beings obviously at risk of hypnosis and people who are not are with out problem hypnotized through the usage of rest strategies. And he presented a advice that have become applicable to the speak. To boost up the device of identifying the color, the fmri display examine out a phrase that modified into basically gibberish.

I underwent a mind check within the route of a Stroop check a few days after my hypnosis session. People who're extra vulnerable to hypnosis, i.E. Folks that provoke conversations with a suggestion, have been additionally higher at making use of the word shade.

To upload insult to damage, there had been moreover discernible versions in thoughts interest. For a few purpose, the thoughts area responsible for deciphering characters remained dormant. It's as although the mind in reality neglected the phrases and did no longer system them as language. Meanwhile, topics were clear as a bell at the place of job. Contrast that with the mind of someone who actively fought hypnosis.

The hypnotic method may additionally additionally have altered the challenge's preceding ideals. This allowed me to apprehend it as a rainbow of colours in place of incomprehensible squiggles. Moreover, neuroscientists have discovered that it prevents the formation of recent recollections.

The player have become hypnotized a week after searching the forty five-minute clip. In order to undergo in mind the movie, I even have come to be recommended to overlook approximately it and achieve some other autograph. After being given the forgetting signal and getting into the useful MRI, the participant though could not preserve in mind the movie's plot. I did consider the capabilities of the room in which I appeared the movie, despite the truth that. Certain areas of the thoughts related to memory had been less active than the nonhypnotic company.

Then, in concept, all you will be capable of don't forget is the habitual scene wherein Luke Skywalker's father seems. Post-hypnotic amnesia describes this situation. It modified into applied as a research model for actual amnesia. It's like having a TBI with out in truth having one.

Some hypnotherapists placed it to use for party tricks, even as others use it as an powerful device for scientific and intellectual dreams.

Surgeons who utilize hypnosis document that it allows their sufferers experience more cushty and comfortable at some stage in the surgical and postoperative strategies. Similarly, it may be used to ease soreness and calm nerves in some unspecified time in the future of tough paintings. Behavioral treatment may be supplemented with hypnosis. Quitting smoking, handling despair, post-disturbing stress contamination, and so on.

Yet hypnosis can not replace medical treatment. Hypnotic guidelines may not be useful for everybody. If so, then hypnosis cannot be denied. You can assume it being real. Despite the fact that hypnosis stays poorly understood through way of psychologists. Hypnosis has been described as attention and expectation through some and as some other state of recognition with the aid of others.

Hypnosis, at maximum, serves as an illustration of the mind's outstanding capabilities. You can't unwind or get a few close-eye in case you are unwilling to. One's angle can be altered to relieve or maybe overlook approximately suffering.

Chapter 7: Extremely rapid hypnosis

People who enter a hypnotic state of affairs upon being subjected to hypnotic concept are said to be in a proper away triggered trance, or proper away hypnosis. Different styles of hypnosis, along side self-hypnosis and conversational hypnosis, in addition to one in every of a type techniques of mind schooling, permit for growing levels of relaxation and suggestibility. Instant guided hypnosis frequently includes a unmarried bodily movement and course from a hypnotherapist or awesome professional practitioner.

The first step in instant prompted hypnosis is commonly getting the state of affairs to just accept to be hypnotized. First-session hypnosis is not commonly accompanied thru right away induction. A person typically goes thru a few different shape of hypnosis first, as a way to obtain a trancelike situation and modify their degree of attention.

When the hypnotist is underneath their private spell, they will advocate their client to undergo fast induction at their subsequent consultation. If the situation is of the same opinion, the hypnotist will commonly train them to go into a trance kingdom at the mere uttering of a motive phrase, regularly found with the useful resource of bodily movements similar to the losing of the issue's hand. This is the time at the same time as the "reason word" is spoken. To offer really one instance, if the hypnotist increases the trouble's hand and says the word "sleep," the scenario will move into hypnosis.

Those interested by studying instant hypnosis normally discover it a easy ability to master, definitely as it's far often shown to be so in amusement and one-of-a-kind hypnosis shows. In fact, notwithstanding the truth that, hypnotists typically do now not discover ways to conduct immediately guided hypnosis until they've studied, practiced, and mastered other hypnosis theories and techniques. Instant hypnosis is a way that takes time and exercising to master, however a expert hypnotist can collect amazing results. An individual's notion inside the hypnotist's competence is crucial to the fulfillment of immediately guided hypnosis.

Many people turn to hypnosis as a way of coping with a massive form of private issues, and proper now guided hypnosis is an powerful device for doing so. It is also less complex for hypnotherapists to use this method all through a consultation. This method shortens the same old duration of inducing an altered nation of recognition. No of the manner long it takes to bring about the trance us of a, the session will usually hobby at the same hassle the purchaser initially came in with.

Chapter 8: Instant hypnosis technique

Many humans, regardless of having a more nuanced information of "hypnosis" and the world of psychology as an entire, no matter the truth that accomplice the time period with the stereotypical television hypnotist.

It's time for mattress...

When I open my eyes inside the morning, I'll be a canine....

It's hypnosis with all the fun stuff taken out of it. Because of this, hypnosis may additionally moreover though have a awful connotation in Japan.

To begin, there may be no issue inside the use of hypnosis to make the alternative individual behave like a dog, react to a sure time period, or be now not succesful to talk a nice quantity.

In assessment, hypnosis therapy hired in psychotherapy regularly consists of regression hypnosis, wherein the affected individual revisits worrying activities from their youth on the way to heal from the trauma and the unsightly activities of the beyond.

Hypnosis is used to "function unconsciously to result in favored changes," as its proponents located it. Recognizing its genesis is critical.

This shape of "hypnosis" moreover consists of a few issue termed "without delay hypnosis," through manner of the way. A client may be placed into a hypnotic trance in a depend of seconds.

Step-through-Step Instructions for Initiating an Instant Hypnotic State

Quick hypnosis may be carried out in some of fantastic tactics. Here, we offer an introduction to immediately hypnosis, and then the patron reminiscences a system very much like that of traditional hypnosis.

We'll skip over arm drop induction, one of the most not unusual strategies to ease someone into speedy hypnosis.

Here are the 6 measures

Place customer's hand in counselor's palm, provide an reason of hypnosis, have consumer interest on counselor's forehead while counselor pushes down on overlapping arms.

You can: • Instantly divert hobby • Enter a hypnotic situation if you want to make customers forget about approximately everything else (country of hypnosis).

The first step is to have them sit down down.

Request that your hypnotized difficulty sit. Put them comfortable through asking them to have a seat.

Your nerves could be targeted at the uncomfortable consultation if you have to sit down down in a immoderate chair with dangling, pressured legs or one which has no lower back, making it more hard to introduce hypnosis.

Provides an proof of hypnosis (issue 2).

Hypnosis cannot be introduced efficaciously if the client is frightened of the way.

A trusting relationship among counselor and client is important for any shape of counseling to succeed, not most effective hypnosis.

You need to ensure the hypnosis treatment you will go through is harmless, might not cause you any damage, and makes its meant effects plain.

Third, the counselor need to take the purchaser's hand and cup it in his or her palm.

The therapist will extend a hand, palm up, to the consumer.

Tell the affected individual to put his or her palm at the counselor's.

④ Focus your interest at the therapist's forehead at the equal time as making use of strain to the interlaced fingers.

Tell your patron to attention at the therapist's forehead. Tell them to stack their fingers and then press down on them.

In evaluation, the counselor facilitates the consumer's downward pushing stress via manner of bringing his hand up from beneath.

Distract the customer's interest right now (5).

This should be executed proper now to divert interest some distance from your palms and forehead. Tell the client to perform a smooth nursery rhyme or repeat his call backwards.

Perform the following 3 moves without delay at the identical time as you wait.

Remove your hand carefully from the interlocking arms. 2. Go to sleep (or say a word that makes you assert "Yes!") Clearly and audibly.

three With the palm of your hand, gently push the patron's torso once more and press at the shoulder.

Your consumer's head or frame may additionally need to suffer extreme damage if you fast input trance and fail to use excessive caution.

Due to the purchaser's loss of ability to offer guide for themselves whilst unconscious, precise hobby want to be paid to the pinnacle and it ought to be supported firmly.

Six Going right into a Deep Trance.

The hypnotic country has taken impact on the purchaser.

The De-Hypnotization Procedure

Just like with each other hypnotist, at the equal time as hypnosis is damaged you're helped to often reawaken.

Use "You come yet again slowly" as an example. I'm calm and satisfied right now. The second I rely to ten, you will be widespread conscious. In the morning, you experience refreshed and cushty. It's expert recognition is "united states."

In addition, counting backwards from ten will help them regain cognizance and feature a examine the commands given.

Summary

Introducing immediate hypnosis may additionally furthermore seem smooth at the begin.

Even if you don't have any experience or education in it, I think you could deliver it a shot; however, I could not propose doing it in reality for a laugh.

It's volatile, it is hard to discover the great to your opponent, and it's far easy to complete which you can't be an effective leader.

As I referred to inside the outset, knowledge why hypnosis exists is vital.

Hypnosis is likewise referred to as a trance or a country of altered focus. Hypnosis is similar to the u . S . A . Of mind wherein one is considering some aspect at the same time as feeling tired proper in advance than falling asleep.

Hypnosis produces a mild, receptive u . S . Of interest. If you maintain an open thoughts and do no longer overanalyze the whole thing, you'll be able to revel in life extra really. The advice of the counselor is properly properly well worth considering.

Short-term hypnosis that, before the entirety look, seems to be within the reap of all people.

Therefore, it is possible that the name of the game to the achievement of speedy hypnosis is in identifying the direction of hypnosis and the patron's meant situation.

Chapter 9: Self Hypnosis, little by little

It is based at the autogenic education approach advanced with the aid of German psychiatrist Dr. JH Schultz in the Thirties for getting organized the autonomic nerves, and the time period "self-hypnosis" refers to the hypnotic nation completed through this exercise.

Self-hypnosis can be used to maintain dormant abilities to the floor, but it is also a facts in and of itself.

These days, it's miles no longer easy to make development.

And a few people are more open to hypnosis than others.

People prone to self-hypnosis.

The reality is that humans regularly mesmerize themselves subconsciously. It's common workout on the identical time as one is inspired through idea. This is a feature of the brain, however susceptibility to suggestion at this degree is referred to as suggestibility.

People who are very suggestible, collectively with folks who declare to have seen ghosts, folks who are as an alternative revolutionary, and those who're regularly defined as "natural," are usually idea to be at risk of autohypnosis. Since autosuggestion is a suggestion to oneself, people who're direct-minded or take delivery of as true with within the impact are much more likely to advantage autohypnosis with the aid of the use of advice by myself.

People who are lots much less inclined to self-hypnotize

In contrast, those who are choosy with their reviews, have hassle articulating their emotions, and do no longer take transport of as authentic with within the efficacy of hypnosis are characterised thru the fact that they may be greater hard to self-hypnotize.

It is stated that folks who do now not have self-hypnosis are much much less vulnerable to be concerned with the aid of the usage of self-hypnosis. In particular, it's far hard to supply a new idea of self-hypnosis to someone who is fascinated about a perception.

Advantages of Hypnosis for Oneself

The crucial benefit of self-hypnosis is the excessive degree of freedom you can advocate to yourself at any 2nd you preference.

after you have got learnt a manner to do it, you can commonly offer yourself the hints you want. Boosting concept, as an instance, might also help people take the steps essential to recognise their targets.

It has the introduced gain of easing pressure and anxiety and helping you note matters in a greater first-rate slight.

Self-hypnosis has its drawbacks.

Conversely, there are risks, and the vital downside of self-hypnosis is that it is hard to have a observe. Many people give up on getting to know self-hypnosis on their private after over and over failing to succeed. Then, you can learn how to use self-hypnosis via way of way of attending a seminar or lecture given via way of a hypnotist who teaches hypnosis.

Self-Hypnosis: How to Do It Yourself

Here are a few guidelines for self-hypnosis. When sporting out self-hypnosis, it's pleasant to accomplish that in a peaceful, private setting. Sitting deeply, as on a couch or futon, permits you to sleep manifestly while hypnotizing yourself. Self-hypnosis can be stepped forward with the resource of stepping into a deep country of sleep in which conscious idea is suspended.

Self-hypnosis includes taking a deep breath, breathing in deeply, closing your eyes, maintaining your breath, after which slowly releasing it. The device need to be repeated 5 instances. Then inform your self time and again that your proper hand is heavy. Follow the same system at the side of your left hand, then your right foot, your left foot, and eventually your head.

Self-hypnosis works terrific if you supply some concept to the affirmations you tell yourself and the highbrow photograph you conjure up of the manner you would like to trade. If you are seeking out to shed kilos, for example, see yourself looking outstanding. If you're feeling sleepy, you could relaxation. Do this every day until you draw near it.

Suggestion for your self

The notion required for self-hypnosis is a word for the picture you recite on your coronary heart, however the belief is important to assume what you need to be.

The key is to frame the belief inside the past worrying or the winning progressive. Please examine that I am not, currently, penning a letter to my future self. Use phrases like "already" or "come to be" to carry to your self that you have already reached your goal.

Make tremendous that a frightening sentence is a pleasant one. The unconscious mind makes it more hard to pick out denial, consequently make certain to make it a tremendous sentence. If you are weight-reduction plan, do now not say "now not fat," as an alternative make it a powerful term which consist of "slender."

Make it right into a photograph-first-class fulfillment sentence like, "I controlled to lose kg" or "I controlled to give up smoking definitely."

Suggestion

Automatic notion describes the device of self-hypnosis. Suggestion is "linguistic stimuli impacting thoughts and perceptions" or "non-verbal (sensory) stimulus". Non-verbal stimuli have an impact on one's "visible enjoy," "auditory feel," "physical experience (tactile experience)," "enjoy of smell," and "sense of flavor," and I apprehend linguistic stimuli, however they imply "I am slender."

Making yourself hungry via making brilliant meals is a suggestive effect of the stimulus. Self-stimulation, or autosuggestion, can be completed through the usage of terms or splendid types of communication.

Subconscious

Self-hypnosis works excellent whilst practiced through a person who has an in depth information of the unconscious mind. Self-hypnosis is a shape of subconscious rewriting.

Should you strive hypnotizing yourself?

One cannot claim that self-hypnosis (or hypnotherapy) is without a doubt threat-loose. Since it might be deceiving and offer weird suggestions if no longer finished by a equipped hypnotist. Bizarre suggestions were related to autonomic illness and intellectual infection inside the beyond.

Practicing self-hypnosis isn't always a recreation; as an alternative, it is a excessive technique of personal boom and trouble-fixing. However, self-hypnosis is usually innocent, supplied that no illogical conclusions are drawn from it. Self-hypnosis is chance-free as long as you stay with thoughts that adhere to "trusting your self" and "understanding the basics of hypnosis."

Chapter 10: Self-hypnosis to sleep as a child

Insomnia, which can be resulting from hassle relieving stress, can make bigger bad emotions.

Through self-hypnosis, you can attain parity of orientation a few of the rational, analytical, and emotional ranges of the thoughts. It's now not possible to make an independent desire even as one's thoughts is have grow to be the alternative manner. Self-hypnosis brings the ones states of recognition into alignment with every different, receives rid of intellectual conflict, and facilitates an goal assessment of every the dominion of mind and the instances. By doing so, you will be able to decorate alternatives in every scenario." (Mr. Hayashi)

Furthermore, self-hypnosis appears to be best for human beings who have hundreds of troubles and characteristic trouble sleeping due to them.

Putting oneself proper right into a hypnotic nation, moreover known as a trance, is similar to placing oneself right right into a state of highbrow lethargy "and is the wonderful feasible manner to wind down earlier than bed.

Never say "Let's do it" because you feel such as you need to. Stress and shortage of sleep are the stop result of your conscious thoughts fighting closer to your unconscious's efforts to find out a way to the state of affairs. Hypnosis When you've got got greater records and a clearer picture of the trouble, you'll enjoy a extremely good deal a great deal less pressured and greater snug." (Mr. Hayashi)

According to Mr. Hayashi, self-hypnosis needs "one-pointed interest" to have the same course of awareness, which naturally promotes hobby. Furthermore, self-hypnosis relieves pressure inside the mind, permitting the subconscious to more with out difficulty create novel mind and glowing insights.

There is proof that it lets in humans carry out higher at the way every day.

■ You can do it beginning these days! Self-hypnosis" technique

Anyone, at any time, can start self-hypnosis, it genuinely is a big plus, in line with Hayashi.

"The key is to unwind from head to toe. Since the mind and frame are interrelated, reducing the stress of the complete frame obviously relaxes the anxiety of the mind" (Mr. Hayashi) (Mr. Hayashi).

Mr. Hayashi proper away showed me a shape of self-hypnosis that even novices may additionally without issue exercise.

Produce hypnosis with one's private volition (autogenic education).

"Autogenic training is a form of self-hypnosis this is carried out as a treatment for highbrow infection and as a manner of intellectual fitness everywhere in the international. This is so due to the fact the crucial capability of self-hypnosis, "one-element attention," is effortlessly found out. Ideal for novices" (Mr. Hayashi)

Autogenic training is nice completed at the identical time as mendacity to your lower decrease again on a futon, genuinely as you will be while you nod off.

<Step 1> The sensation of getting heavy hands or legs is recommended thru the phrase "heavy arms / legs."

Start thru saying "Heavy right arm.... Heavy proper arm..." out loud for 30 seconds right away. If your dominant arm is your left, say "left arm." After 30 seconds, revel in the load of the suggesting right arm at the same time as repeating "I revel in definitely peaceful...".

Repeat the machine of swiftly turning your attention to the possibility arm and repeating the belief in the order of right arm left arm right leg left leg, and maintain doing so until you revel in a sensation of heaviness. This need to be performed regardless of whether or not or no longer or no longer you are now experiencing a experience of heaviness. When you've got were given got reached the point wherein you can consciously revel in the limbs' weight with the beneficial useful resource of concept, pass straight away to the subsequent diploma.

"

Do not make the mistake of looking to make oneself heavier or loosen up within the in the meantime. Try to generate a weaker united states of america of the us genuinely with suggestive strength as you honestly communicate. So, allow's get to it. If you sense a hint heavier than normal, it's far because of the truth your muscle tissues have calmed down, which has launched stress to your blood vessels. It may also take some try, however in case you grasp this degree, the subsequent steps will pass smoothly." ...(Mr. Hayashi)

<Step 2> Implications of limb warm temperature Arms and legs are saved heat.

Again, for approximately 30 seconds, trace at "heat," after which, at the same time as pronouncing, "feeling quite tranquil...", enjoy the warm temperature of the indicated phase. To get toasty, you need to hold doing this, beginning together together with your right arm, then moving in your left arm, then your proper leg, and in the end your left leg. When your limbs experience comfortable, circulate at once to the following diploma.

"Step one in raising core frame temperature is growing blood go together with the go with the flow. Let's pork up and solidify that feeling through perception. When you could feel warm temperature, you could relaxation both physically and mentally. You want to be in a country of agitation." (Mr. Hayashi)

<Step three> Recommended coronary heart fee: the silent beating of the coronary coronary heart.

After continuing with step 2, recommend that "the heart beats quietly" for about 30 seconds, and in the long run experience the coronary coronary heart beat gently as you assert "I experience exceedingly relaxed..." Let's do this. If you are feeling calm internal, you're organized for step four.

* If your coronary coronary heart isn't as much as it, go with the flow on to step 4.

Tip for regulating your respiratory: "Breathing is simple."

After moving at once to Step three, I spent about 30 seconds teasing, "I am breathing very pleasantly.... I am breathing softly and slowly," earlier than in the end choosing, "I sense honestly comfortable." Just take a deep breath and pride inside the peace it brings. Once you have were given executed a country of quiet respiration, proceed to Step five.

* If you be via a respiratory problem, you can pass ahead to step 5.

"By lightly beating your heart, your breathing becomes proportionately tranquil. It's difficult to try and sluggish your respiratory down, so do no longer do it." Mr. Hayashi, directly to step 5: "heat stomach" as a metaphor for inner warmness.

After intending to step four, inform yourself that your stomach is warm temperature for spherical thirty seconds, after which ultimately feel the warmth of your stomach on the equal time as mentioning "I feel particularly relaxed..." If you experience your tummy is warmth, maintain to step 6.

<Step 6> Consequences of a Cold Headache Implications: "The forehead is cold".

Finally, after 30 seconds of stating "I feel extremely calm..." and specializing inside the loosen up of your forehead, flow into at once to step 6.

"It is said that once your forehead feels cold, you're at the excellent nation of your body and your thoughts is perfectly normal. The strain is absolutely absorbed, accordingly it's miles the most acceptable united states of america for analyzing and operating". Mr. Hayashi recommends doing steps 1–6 for five–10 minutes every day, as quickly as upon waking up and another time earlier than bed. Doing this right before mattress will make you enjoy cushty and prepared for sleep.

"Self-hypnosis" that relieves tension nicely and complements sleep incredible. By taking some time without work, you could recharge your frame and mind, allowing you to do better artwork on every occasion you return. If you want to "enjoy true" but it does no longer artwork, why no longer start thru feeling "a country of rest on your mind and frame" on this manner?

Chapter 11: Age Regression

When thinking about quick self-hypnosis, you need to inquire of yourself: What is the significance of time to your lifestyles? How do you bear in mind it?

Everyone has a top notch attitude on matters. Where do you photograph your self for your records if I ask you to visualize yourself?

Do you believe you studied it'll probably be proper at the back of you? / Do you believe you studied it will in all likelihood be proper within the once more of you? Or do you think it's far off to the side of you in your creativeness? Or probably it's miles at an mindset.

When I ask you to take into account the future, do you image it in the the front of you or to the aspect of you?

As we circulate from the past into the future, at the same time as you consider the passage of time, do you photo it strolling up your frame or to as a minimum one facet of it? It's feasible that neither of these thoughts enters your thoughts in any respect. It's possible that you could recognize or revel in it in a very splendid manner.

When you are with a lovable girl for 2 hours, you may feel similar to the time has flown with the resource of in a flash. However, in case you sit on a heat burner for one minute, you could keep in mind which you have been there for 2 hours. This is the idea of relativity: Einstein

How do you picture your self while you have been more younger? Age regression and instantaneous self-hypnosis are approaches to find out this question.

You have to recognise that there may be no accurate or wrong option to this puzzle. Regarding this issue count, every folks holds a completely particular element of view.

It may seem that nearly everybody area the past each behind us or to at the least one element, and we area the destiny each within the the the front dad and mom or on the opposite thing.

Just supply some belief to that for a 2d.

Put your palms over your eyes and try to conjure up what it became like again then, while following the route of your non-public particular chronology. To start, consider some thing that happened the day in advance than.

Then ultimate week. Then, the month earlier than final. After that, twelve months within the past. When we have been five years older and so forth.

Now that I keep in mind it, the ones items were all in severa places as soon as I became thinking about them, were not they? And there may be no question in my mind that they were of various sizes.

Instantaneous Self-Hypnosis and the Regression of One's Own Age Age Progression

That's one of the ways our minds assist us make revel in of the passage of time. Now, supply a few perception to the future years. Continue with the same form of workout.

Close your eyes again. Consider a undertaking that you may maximum possibly do the day after tomorrow.

Consider an hobby that you can take part in at some point of the approaching week. After that, internal some months (in all likelihood a vacation). Then maintain in mind what's going to seem inside the future. Check out how far it's far going.

Again, the one of a kind pics you create can be of diverse sizes and in notable locations. Additional blessings embody age regression and rapid self-hypnosis.

Now which you have your chronology set, you could positioned it to appropriate use to result in a country of instantaneous self-hypnosis in your self.

To start, allowing your self to clearly waft spherical your timeline every so often may be a lovely manner to loosen up and unwind.

Maybe you want you may flow lower back in time and relive a pleased memory with a loved one who is no longer with you, or perhaps you need you may tour into the destiny and note what you might be capable of accumulate.

Imagine a extended road that stretches as a long manner as the attention can view, and make it extensive sufficient so that you can consist of the whole thing that you need to perform alongside the manner. Do this on every occasion you don't forget the future.

When you replicate in your existence, try to journey as an extended way once more as possible, all of the way to the primary recollection you may recall. It's possible that you'll be greatly surprised with the aid of the usage of how a exceptional deal you can don't forget.

Carry out the interest inside the aforementioned way, but no longer earlier than you have got were given examine all the instructions.

Marking the winning while concurrently regressing via the a long term via on the spot self-hypnosis

Close your eyes. Imagine which you are at the winning on the spot on your timeline and that you are reputation there. Put a huge flagpole in your mind's eye and region it on the floor surely subsequent to in which you're status so that you do not lose your bearings.

Then, ascend into the air above your chronology so that you can observe its continuation into the imminent years.

Then you ought to face it from the opportunity course and bear in mind the way it reaches all the manner back to the time of your begin (or maybe beyond if you need).

Now, start to slowly go with the waft backwards alongside your timeline, searching first on the maximum current events to your existence after which, as you flow into backwards, gradually viewing and recalling greater a long way off recollections. When you gain the give up of your timeline, you will have experienced everything that has befell to you all through your entire existence.

While you're doing this, assume decrease again to the emotions you have been experiencing inside the in the meantime. Think once more to the odors which is probably linked to the recollections. While you have got a look at the photographs, you must amplify them and colorize them as you pass.

Because the thoughts employs all of these senses to keep in mind reminiscences, you will be astonished through even more memories a excellent manner to start to pour in as you still use every of your senses on this manner.

They are all tucked up deep interior your very personal being. It's as clean as giving them what they need as a praise.

After you have got retraced your steps to the thing wherein you can keep in mind the sports of nowadays, hold to go together with the go with the flow once more to the prevailing in a sluggish and constant manner till you be aware the flagpole standing on the ground. After that, make your manner all the manner all the manner right down to the floor cautiously, and unwind.

If you carry out this exercising multiple times on separate days, you can discover that on every occasion a latest memory will floor. This is a few factor you can assume to take place. When you install greater try, you may discover greater records.

Conquering a trouble via the usage of age regression and immediate self-hypnosis

Imagine for a 2nd that you'll be wanting to stand and triumph over an impediment sooner or later within the now not too some distance flung destiny. It might also moreover need to go to some aspect the least bit. It need to have some component to do at the side of your system, a carrying occasion, an examination, or maybe an interview for a brand new method. Of direction, the ones are just a few examples to go through in thoughts.

Put your eyes out and think in your existence's activities. Once you have got got installation the existing via using planting the flag at the floor, you may ascend above the timeline and begin to go with the flow backwards.

It's viable that at one component within the beyond you conquered a trouble that became similar to this one. We have all, subsequently in our lives, triumphed in opposition to adversity and warfare, no matter the fact that the instances might not had been exactly the equal.

Now, let yourself go along with the go with the glide again in time to right before you faced that obstacle. See the way you regarded. Feel the manner you felt. Pay hobby to what you have got heard. Imagine taking over the trouble and developing successful from the experience.

Float relatively in advance of the component in time even as you efficiently overcome the impediment. Recall the exceptional sense of fulfillment you had at that point. Take look at of the techniques you employed to triumph over the obstacle.

It is essential to hold in thoughts that when you have accrued all your resources, it may not were as tough as you imagined it is probably.

Now, allow's come back to the right right here and now. Keep shifting the cursor over the timeline in the perfect path. Imagine which you have floated into the future quickly earlier than the hassle that you may must confront.

Put the sources from the previous try once more into play. Keep in thoughts all the sparkling records and assets that you have acquired in view that then, and gather all of it collectively.

Now see yourself making use of those assets, going through the difficulty, and successfully overcoming it.

Consider the moments right away following your fulfillment and pay attention to how notable you appearance and the way nicely you experience within the ones moments.

Whenever you experience prepared, go along with the flow again to the proper here and now after which make your manner all of the way right all the way down to the floor.

Regression at some degree in the ages and instantaneous self-hypnosis also are viable.

When carried out on this manner for the cause of short self-hypnosis, your timeline is an top notch tool for attaining each calm and success.

When you're truely immersed for your imagination, not simplest are you clearly hypnotized, but you also are in reality inquisitive about the enjoy. This is the exquisite method to gather fast self-hypnosis. It is an approach that I hire, and it's miles one which I strongly advocate to others.

What exactly are hypnotism and NLP, besides?

Because hypnotism is an powerful approach for presenting advantages to as a minimum one's subconscious mind, neuro-linguistic programming (NLP) and hypnosis in the meanwhile are often used collectively.

What precisely is hypnotism, then? Unfortunately, level hypnotists and films like "The Ipcress File," among different things, have contributed to the substantial perception that it's far feasible to control the minds of various people to the factor wherein they may be made to seem silly on degree or, in the worst case situation, programmed to homicide.

None of these interpretations represents the reality, the complete fact, or some component even close to it.

The fierce competition of these with common intellect has always been a undertaking for terrific spirits.

Albert Einstein

Hypnosis and Neuro-Linguistic ProgrammingThe Stages of Hypnosis

If your most effective experience with hypnosis and NLP comes from watching theatrical hypnotists carry out on television, you in all likelihood have no longer visible what happens in a stay overall performance even as the hypnotist asks for volunteers to assist him or her earlier than the show starts offevolved offevolved offevolved. If that is your great exposure to hypnosis and NLP, you is probably amazed thru what happens.

If you ever had any aim of becoming one in each of them, then you definately are nicely aware that you acquire right here perilously close to passing out at some point of the opposition for the quantity while a swarm of extroverts rushed the degree inside the hopes of having determined on.

If the hypnotist informed the bulk of them to strut approximately the degree clucking like a bird at the same time as waving their fingers, the reality is that the hypnotist could no longer want to hypnotize them first considering the fact that they'll do it anyway, even without being hypnotized.

Hypnosis and Neuro-Linguistic Programming: Adjusting the Target Audience

Stage hypnotists are acquainted with studying their target market with a purpose to decide who in the crowd is most in all likelihood to conform with their commands and who will no longer, in addition to who may be the very nice to control.

If a person claims that they do no longer don't forget some thing from the immediately they have been hypnotized till the time they decrease lower lower back to their seat in the theater, you have to take their phrase for it with a huge grain of salt.

That degree of unconsciousness is reached both whilst a person is useless or while they may be extraordinarily slumbering. Those who commit themselves seriously to the exercising of hypnotism and NLP are familiar with this idea.

Daydreaming with Hypnosis and NLP Techniques

It is feasible that it might be more accurate to represent hypnotism as a type of reverie, it in reality is while the thoughts becomes divided and one half of of you operates on autopilot while the other a part of you enters a dreamy u . S ..

In this context, we speak to the sports activities of both the aware or the unconscious mind (some say "subconscious").

It is a beneficial way to provide an explanation for the technique, even though the mind isn't in truth split in in any huge sense.

Hypnosis and Neuro-Linguistic Programming: Can you hypnotize others?

Printed in the USA
CPSIA information can be obtained
at www.ICGtesting.com
LVHW010315161023
761181LV00003B/202

9 781998 927166